# CONQUER YOUR **IMPOSTER**

# CONQUER YOUR IMPOSTER

Dismantle the fear that undermines your success.

Unlock your true potential.

Free yourself from Imposter Syndrome for good.

ALISON SHAMIR

First published in 2025 by Dean Publishing
PO Box 119
Mt. Macedon, Victoria, 3441
Australia
deanpublishing.com

Cataloguing-in-Publication Data
National Library of Australia
Title: Conquer Your Imposter
ISBN: 978-1-925452-97-6
Category: Self-help/personal development

The views and opinions expressed in this book are those of the author and do not necessarily reflect the official policy or position of any other agency, publisher, organization, employer, medical body or company. Assumptions made in the analysis are not reflective of the position of any entity other than the author(s)—and, these views are always subject to change, revision, and rethinking at any time.

This book is educational only and not intended as a substitute for the medical advice of physicians or psychological evaluations by professionals. Imposter Syndrome is not a clinically diagnosed illness and the author is not diagnosing but merely giving an opinion from her own research and lived experiences.

The reader should regularly consult a trusted physician in matters relating to their personal health, particularly with respect to any symptoms that may require diagnosis or medical attention. Some topics within this book may be confronting for some readers, discretion is advised.

The author has recreated events from her memory and experience. The author has ensured that the names, personal characteristics of individuals, characteristics of organizations and details of events and locations in this book have been changed to disguise the identities or protect the privacy of others. Any resulting resemblance to persons or organizations is entirely coincidental and unintentional. The author's intent is to only offer understanding, inspiration, and education to others regarding Imposter Syndrome.

Your mental, physical, and emotional health are vital and need to be discussed with your own medical professionals. The author and its related entities will not be liable for any loss or damage (financial or otherwise) that may arise out of your improper use of, or reliance on, the content of this resource. You accept sole responsibility for the outcomes if you choose to adopt and/or use the ideas, concepts, ideologies, philosophies, and opinions within this book.

The author, publisher or organizations are not to be held responsible for misuse, reuse, recycled and cited and/or uncited copies of content within this book by others.

To my father, Mile—for giving me life
and saving my life.

I wouldn't be who I am without your
unconditional support. This is the
beginning of a new journey, and I wish
I could put this book in your hands,
but I know you're with me in spirit.

I love you and miss you every day.

A note to readers:

This book briefly references personal experiences with domestic and family violence, suicide, and an eating disorder in its early chapters. These mentions are woven into the narrative with care and respect but may be difficult for some. Your well-being matters and I want you to feel supported and empowered.

Thank you for joining me in Conquer Your Imposter™

Alison

# CONTENTS

# INTRODUCTION

# YOU ARE NOT ALONE

You picked up this book because you're a high performer who strives for high achievement, even if you don't want to admit it to yourself. But you carry a secret, and there are millions of intelligent, talented, qualified, and accomplished people just like you around the world who are doing the same.

At times, you believe you're an intellectual fraud, plagued by a fear that you'll soon be "found out" or "exposed" as not being good enough, smart enough, worthy enough. You feel this way despite overwhelming evidence that proves you deserve your position and accomplishments (you know, all your certificates, awards, qualifications, work experience, titles, medals).

Sound familiar?

This experience has a name—Imposter Phenomenon, commonly referred to as Imposter Syndrome. But where does this phenomenon come from? Why can't you own the success you've earned? And what power do you hold to change it?

I answer all of this and much more in *Conquer Your Imposter*™, your personal guide to understanding and overcoming the shadow that is Imposter Syndrome—and it *can* be overcome. I'm living proof of that, as are the countless clients I've helped over the years.

This book is a journey of powerful self-discovery. It's about peeling back the layers of your story, understanding the fabric of your belief system, and reconstructing a more authentic, empowered version of yourself. You are not one-dimensional, and neither is your Imposter Syndrome. While you may never have ultimate control over your environment, the one thing you can always steer is yourself, your choices, the way you speak to yourself, and the actions you take.

You have the power to retrain your brain to be your greatest ally. This book will guide you in transforming self-sabotage into new habits that pave the way to the success you truly want and deserve.

Your Imposter Syndrome is not something you have to live with.

It's time to dismantle the fear that undermines your success.

Unlock your true potential.

Free yourself from Imposter Syndrome for good.

# CHAPTER ONE

"When you free yourself from Imposter Syndrome, you not only achieve success, but you finally own it, enjoy it, and celebrate it."

—Alison Shamir

# THE IMPOSTER PHENOMENON

## THE 70 PERCENT CLUB

In the corridors of the corporate world, the hallowed halls of academia, and even on the glitzy stages of celebrity, there lurks a shadow. This shadow isn't cast by any tangible object, but rather by a pervasive, internal belief: "I am not deserving. I am a fraud."

Welcome, you're part of an exclusive and often secretive group. I know it sounds like a spy movie, college sorority, or like we should be wearing gold pins or have a special handshake. Alas, none of those are needed to be in this special club, reserved for those of us who are talented, intelligent, capable, qualified individuals yet ignore all of the evidence to support this. Instead, we believe we're actually intellectual frauds on the verge of being "found out."

I am, of course, talking about Imposter Syndrome, or Imposter Phenomenon. So, is it a syndrome or a phenomenon? I'll come back to that soon, but first I want you to know how special and far-reaching this club is.

It not only includes talented, intelligent, capable, and qualified individuals like you, but also well-known business icons, poets, actors, writers, award winners, celebrities, professors, CEOs, and sports stars. Former First Lady Michelle Obama, actress Emma Watson, and even the great Albert Einstein have all been members of this club. At some point during their careers, they felt that they were swindlers and frauds, waiting to be exposed.

For many, the feelings associated with Imposter Syndrome can be both baffling and isolating. How can someone with a trophy cabinet, wall, or social media page adorned with accolades or a résumé packed with accomplishments still feel like they're on the verge of being exposed as a fraud? You're about to find out.

## MY TOXIC RELATIONSHIP WITH IMPOSTER SYNDROME

Firstly, however, I have a confession to make. I used to be a member of this club. In fact, Imposter Syndrome's shadow loomed large over me for a decade. We had a toxic on-again, off-again relationship. That was, until 2013 when we officially began our breakup, or, shall I say, we consciously uncoupled. When a debilitating panic attack struck me at work, I didn't know what was happening to me, but the event completely changed the course of my life and led me to where I am today.

Although I had been unknowingly battling Imposter Syndrome for years, I didn't know what I was experiencing. I didn't have a label for it, and I certainly didn't have a solution, so I continued to suffer throughout most of my working days. I didn't realize that something was seriously wrong. After all, a bit of self-doubt is normal, right? Some would even say it's healthy because it keeps us humble. However, the thoughts and feelings that led me to experience a crippling panic attack right before an important meeting stemmed from more than just self-doubt. They were, as I later learned, the hallmarks of Imposter Syndrome.

By late 2013, I was 30 years old, and I had built a formidable corporate career, predominantly in the technology sector plus three years in media and publishing, holding multiple leadership roles. At the time, I was working for a large US company, which meant plenty of travel and a generous salary. On paper, I was living the corporate dream—so why did it feel so wrong?

On the outside, everything looked great—I was strong and successful. However, beneath the surface, I was at constant war with an enemy I didn't understand or have a label for. When we don't understand the problem, overcoming it is near-impossible. Personally, I didn't understand how big the issue was, so, as many do, I chose to ignore it. What could possibly go wrong …?

As long as I kept up a positive outer appearance, people saw me as calm, confident, like a woman with her shit together—and I *did* have my shit together. I was performing well, was outwardly confident, and was leading a successful team, but on the inside I was suffering. I felt that I wasn't good enough or smart enough to hold my position or represent the company. I lived in constant fear that my boss would call me to say, "Alison, we shouldn't have given you this job," which matched the voice in my head that kept saying, *You don't deserve to be here. You shouldn't be leading the team. You're going to blow it, and then they'll know you're a fraud.* Essentially, I had what's known as high-functioning anxiety, and over time the constant tension and fear took a toll on my mental health. Most days, I went to work genuinely scared that today would be the day I got outed as an intellectual phony.

Over the course of several months, the anxiety built up to a point where I could no longer contain it. It had nowhere to go but out. When the panic attack struck, I was in the office, preparing for an important meeting scheduled for later that day. I had never experienced a panic attack before, and I didn't know what was happening to me. Honestly, I thought I was having a complete mental breakdown. I rushed to the bathroom, and thankfully it was empty, so I didn't need to explain myself to anyone—not that I was capable of an explanation.

Even after over a decade, I remember that panic attack like it was yesterday. The feeling of absolute loss of control. Sweating profusely. The walls closing in on me. I didn't realize at the time—hindsight is a wonderful thing—that it had been building up for months. I just learned to deal with high-functioning anxiety, and I ignored the symptoms until I pushed my brain and body so far they began to shut down. Suddenly, my mental struggle had become physical, and I crashed—I crashed *hard*.

In a couple of hours, I was supposed to lead my team into a big meeting. But how could I lead anyone now? I had lost control, and I didn't know why. *What's happening to me?* I felt so alone and ashamed that everyone would finally find out I had been fooling them. The jig was up. Clearly, I was falling apart under pressure, and my boss would realize he had hired the wrong person and would send me packing. It was the same catastrophic thinking I lived with daily, but it had reached a new level of intensity.

Somehow, after sweating through my shirt, I managed to suck it up, compose myself, and leave the bathroom in a less distressed state. I even managed to lead the team in that important meeting as if nothing had happened. But something *had* happened, and I couldn't ignore it anymore. Clearly, something was wrong, so I went on a desperate hunt for a solution.

At the time, I didn't know that Imposter Syndrome existed, but I wanted answers, and I wanted them *yesterday*. However, I couldn't ask anyone for help because I was fearful of admitting the secret I had held for so long. I was ashamed of finally being exposed as a phony. Essentially, I was being restrained by my own sense of shame. It was a tough situation, but one I was determined to understand.

Shame is one of the strongest emotions attached to Imposter Syndrome, and, as I learned, it can prevent us from seeking help. So, I went it alone, spending late nights hunting all over the internet for answers and adding lack of sleep to the mix, which didn't help my anxiety levels. But I was on a mission and if you ask anyone who knows me, they'll tell you that, once I fix my mind on something, I'm relentless—failure isn't an option. In my search for answers, I google doctored myself in every way possible (who else is guilty of this?) until an article jumped off the screen at me. The article described my experience perfectly. *Whoa …* Finally, I learned that what I was experiencing had a name and, to my relief, I wasn't alone. In fact, I was part of a pretty big club.

I read article after article, study after study, immersing myself in the subject. Through my relentless research, I learned that I couldn't outrun Imposter Syndrome. No matter how successful I got, I would still feel that constant fear and anxiety, unless I addressed the problem at its core.

My journey to understanding and, importantly, *overcoming* Imposter Syndrome had begun.

Fast-forward to today, and I believe I can achieve anything I set my mind to. But, as you can see, that wasn't always the case. My path in life hasn't been easy. For my entire life, I've been effectively in the minority. As a little girl, I knew I was gay. In fact, my earliest memory is being around nine years old and knowing I was "different."

I had a difficult childhood. When I was four years old, my parents went through a horrific divorce. It was about as bad as it gets—the worst of the worst. It tore our family apart. My mother was the catalyst.

To put it plainly, she wasn't a nice person. She ended up abandoning me and my two brothers before returning to take me from the family home, even though I had a close relationship with my father. She then subjected me to years of mental and physical abuse—not just from her but from her new husbands too (she married twice more). During this time, I suffered a lot, but there *is* a silver lining. I also built a lot of resilience, which I carry with me to this day. Unfortunately, the struggle didn't end with childhood.

In my early twenties, when I entered full-time work, I was the youngest on my team, and I was forced to navigate bullying and harassment by male managers and sexual harassment from clients. I've often been the only woman, person of my age, or gay person in the room. Over the years, I've seen and experienced a lot. I know what it's like to feel like an Imposter, like I don't belong in the room. I also know how to overcome it, and, by reading this book, you will too.

# YOU'RE NOT IMAGINING IT

At the time of writing, it has been nearly fifty years since Dr. Pauline Rose Clance and Dr. Suzanne Imes coined the term Impostor Phenomenon in 1974 and later produced their 1978 paper "The Imposter Phenomenon in High Achieving Women: Dynamics and Therapeutic Intervention."[1]

Their studies, which primarily focused on high-achieving women, unveiled a consistent pattern: despite possessing ample qualifications and accomplishments, many women felt like intellectual phonies.

Dr. Clance's and Dr. Imes's pivotal 1978 study finally gave a label and definition to a problem so many people face:

> The term impostor phenomenon is used to designate an internal experience of intellectual phonies, which appears to be particularly prevalent and intense among a select sample of high achieving women. Certain early family dynamics and later introjection of societal sex-role stereotyping appear to contribute significantly to the development of the impostor phenomenon. Despite outstanding academic and professional accomplishments, women who experience the imposter phenomenon persist in believing that they are really not bright and have fooled anyone

> who thinks otherwise. Numerous achievements, which one might expect to provide ample object evidence of superior intellectual functioning, do not appear to affect the impostor belief.[2]

On the surface, it seems counterintuitive. How could someone who has achieved genuine success possibly feel like an Imposter? Shouldn't the repeated validation of continual achievement be enough to break free of the phenomenon? Like I said, you can't outrun Imposter Syndrome—the solution isn't that simple. Why? Because those of us who experience Imposter Syndrome don't properly internalize our success. Instead, we dismiss it as luck, chance, or charm, or attribute it to other people, third parties, or anything other than our own hard work. We deflect, rather than accept.

Although the initial studies focused on women, as conversations and research expanded it became glaringly obvious that this wasn't a "women-only" issue; it was an inclusive, all-gender phenomenon. More recent research has documented these feelings of inadequacy among men, women, and gender-nonconforming individuals in many professional settings and among multiple ethnic and racial groups.[3] While Imposter Syndrome doesn't discriminate—it actually affects men and women almost equally—different genders have different ways of coping with the experience. For example, men tend to try to "push through," which can lead to mental health issues, whereas women tend to let it stunt their careers, as they shy away from opportunities, such as promotions.[4]

Despite being first documented by psychologists and commonly referred to as a "syndrome," it may surprise you to learn that Imposter Syndrome isn't a recognized psychiatric disorder. That's right—it isn't actually listed in the American Psychiatric Association's (APA's) *Diagnostic and Statistical Manual (DSM)*, although some researchers have recommended its inclusion to assist health professionals provide systemized treatment.[5] So, if it isn't a syndrome, what is it? At its core, Imposter Syndrome is a fear based experience that affects a person's perception of themselves and their success. It's not a one-size-fits-all feeling either, meaning that how I have experienced Imposter Syndrome might not be the same as how you have experienced it. However, there will be some commonalities among us all, which we'll explore throughout this book.

For some, Imposter Syndrome is something that shows up regularly, even every day. For others, it can come in key moments of progress, transition, or change. Dr. Clance developed her own test and scale to understand whether someone's Imposter experience is low, moderate, frequent, or intense. You can access the test via her website (www.paulineroseclance.com/pdf/IPTestandscoring.pdf) to determine exactly where you sit on the Imposter scale.[6] Knowing the severity of your Imposter Syndrome is an important step in conquering it.

You might be asking—if it's not actually a syndrome, why has Imposter Syndrome become the widely accepted label? After all, Imposter Phenomenon is the original term. To answer the question, let's take a quick walk through history …

As mentioned, Dr. Clance and Dr. Imes investigated and labeled the phenomenon in their game-changing 1978 paper. However, somewhere along the line, the terminology got switched, and the new label became mainstream. Dr. Imes herself has implied that the term "Imposter Syndrome" is inaccurate and potentially misleading.[7] So, how did the switch to a less ideal label occur? The first known use of the term "Imposter Syndrome" appeared in 1981 in *Vogue*, a popular fashion and lifestyle magazine. From there, it took off, permeating 80s pop culture, and stuck, much to the disappointment of Dr. Clance and Dr. Imes. In the same year, the term made its way into academic literature, and the chance to correct the record had passed.[8] Imposter Syndrome was here to stay.

Of course, knowing what I know, I was met with a bit of a dilemma when writing this book. Do I continue to use a popular yet inaccurate term? Or do I switch to the correct yet lesser-known label? It was a tough choice. Due to the popular and widespread usage of "syndrome," for the sake of clarity and consistency, I've chosen to use the more common name, "Imposter Syndrome," throughout this book. With that said, I encourage you to use whichever terminology you prefer.

While both terms originated in the United States, the feelings associated with Imposter Syndrome are universal—it doesn't discriminate. No matter your gender, race, or ethnicity, Imposter Syndrome can strike if the conditions are right. A review of eleven studies that investigated the prevalence of Imposter Syndrome in minority groups found that the phenomenon is indeed widespread among African-, Asian-, and Latino-American college students.[9] Clearly, we're dealing with a *human* issue that spans continents, races, ethnic groups, and genders.

At some point in their lives, an estimated 70 percent of people globally have felt the weight of this phenomenon and had its shadow cast over their achievements and success.[10] In some groups, the prevalence of the phenomenon may be even higher. For example, a KPMG study found that 75 percent of female executives across a range of industries experienced Imposter Syndrome throughout their careers.[11] Pinpointing a firm statistic for the broader population has proved difficult. One comprehensive meta-analysis of 62 studies found the number to be anywhere from 9 to 82 percent.[12] However, it's important to note that not all research, surveys, or studies are created equal, with some failing to properly highlight the true definition of Imposter Syndrome, thus making the data inaccurate. Few things in life are clear-cut, and as experts we've largely come to accept the 70 percent figure.

Whether we hail from Tokyo or Toronto, Sydney or San Francisco, Bangalore or Buenos Aires, Lagos or London, the fear of being exposed as an intellectual fraud looms large for the majority of us. Yet we feel like we're alone because, often, no one talks about it. With deeply rooted emotions, such as shame, guilt, and embarrassment, heavily tied to Imposter Syndrome, we tend to stay quiet to protect ourselves from experiencing these emotions.

However, as the research suggests, it's a big club, and the majority of us have experienced, or will experience, Imposter Syndrome at some point in our lives. We're not as alone as we think we are.

Imposter Syndrome is older than I am, so you can imagine my frustration when "internet experts" attempt to dwindle it down to a punchy and misleading article designed as clickbait. It's a serious set of feelings that can greatly impact an individual's career and life. There's no need to fear it, because it can be understood and dismantled, but it most certainly deserves serious attention.

## The Imposter Evolution

**1978**

Dr. Clance and Dr. Imes coin the term "Impostor Phenomenon" in their first paper.

**1980s**

The initial studies expand, revealing that this isn't a women-only experience. The first documented case of the word "syndrome" instead of phenomenon appears.

**1990s**

The corporate world starts recognizing and addressing the impacts of Imposter Syndrome, especially in high achieving professionals.

**2000s**

Research shows the global prevalence of Imposter Syndrome, debunking the myth of it being a Western phenomenon.

**2010s**

Conversations around Imposter Syndrome diversify, highlighting its effects across different gender identities, professional realms, and cultural backgrounds. We start to explore the environmental factors that trigger these feelings.

**2020s**

The narrative emphasizes the link between Imposter Syndrome and mental well-being, urging for a more holistic approach to its understanding and management. Links to mental illness conditions are documented.

## IMPOSTER SYNDROME IS BEING BASTARDIZED

In the digital age, where information spreads at the speed of light, it has become easier than ever to disseminate both truth and falsehood. At the time of writing this book, the internet is teeming with false information about Imposter Syndrome. Misunderstandings muddy the mind, making it challenging for those who are genuinely grappling with Imposter Syndrome to find clarity. Like any topic that's global in nature and impacts so many people, it becomes open to dissection by the personal opinion brigade.

While the old adage tells us "we are all entitled to an opinion," we also have to be aware that voicing our opinions about serious issues that are heavily tied to mental health and mental illness can have a lasting and negative impact on those who may be truly suffering. We must tread carefully.

The nuances of Imposter Syndrome are being overshadowed by myths and overgeneralizations, often perpetuated by those who lack a comprehensive understanding of the phenomenon or, worse, simply want to push their own agendas and get eyeballs on their content by saying things that are deliberately controversial and untrue. In a world where attention is currency, we're unfortunately seeing this more and more.

So, it's time to put some of these misconceptions to bed.

### Imposter Syndrome only affects women.

As you know, we've already debunked this one. No gender is immune to the feelings of intellectual fraudulence (despite evidence of one's accomplishments and success), which is the hallmark of Imposter Syndrome. But how and why it shows up from gender to gender can vary.

Despite the initial study focusing on women, how Imposter Syndrome affects men has been discussed since the 1980s. While results of past studies have been mixed, with some research suggesting little variation between genders, a 2024 meta-analysis found that women tend to experience Imposter Syndrome slightly more than men. However, the main takeaway is still the same: Imposter Syndrome can affect anyone of any gender.[13]

### Imposter Syndrome = a fancy name for self-doubt.

While self-doubt is a symptom, equating the two is a gross oversimplification. Imposter Syndrome dives much deeper, often rooted in long-held limiting beliefs about one's self-worth and value. It has you questioning yourself and your identity first before you question what you "do."

Psychotherapist and fellow Imposter Syndrome expert Stevon Lewis shares his view:

> "Self-Doubt is what I would categorize as a healthy negative emotion/experience like worry, anger, or sadness. Impostor Syndrome is the unhealthy version like anxiety, rage, and depression would be for the aforementioned healthy negative emotions. Self-Doubt gets us to slow down in situations where we might not have exhibited mastery so that we don't fall on our faces and usually disappears once we've exhibited some level of mastery. Impostor Syndrome doesn't disappear despite there being overwhelming evidence to support that someone has what it takes."

While everyone experiences self-doubt—it's a natural part of the learning process—Imposter Syndrome is a whole other beast.

Dr. Clance sums it up perfectly:

> "The experience I was trying to describe was more specific than mere self-doubt; it was a fear of being found out, revealed for what I really was."[14]

**Imposter Syndrome is a superpower in disguise.**

Some believe that feeling like an Imposter can drive individuals to work harder; hence it's a "blessing in disguise." However, the stress and anxiety that accompany these feelings are far from beneficial.

Feeling like an intellectual fake, phony, or fraud isn't a good source of motivation because it keeps your body in a constant fear state of fight, flight, freeze, or fawn. Working harder, pushing yourself to "prove yourself" or "outrun" your Imposter Syndrome is a dangerous pursuit—because you can't outrun this experience. Sure, you can try to convince yourself that these feelings keep you "on the ball" or "hungry for success," but these types of thoughts still lure you into a false reality. At the end of the day, you're doing all of this—rather than standing in your authentic strengths and identity, knowing your true worth—because you still feel like a fraud or not good enough. You don't feel worthy or deserving of your position or accomplishments.

It's time to stop crediting your Imposter Syndrome for your success. This creates a false sense of identity and self-worth. You don't need these feelings to be successful or to present and perform at your best.

The notion that Imposter Syndrome is a "performance enhancer" or can make you "more effective" got a renewed push in 2022 with the publication of research in the *Academy of Management Journal*. The study found a link between Imposter Syndrome and interpersonal effectiveness in the workplace, meaning those suffering Imposter thoughts may exhibit superior interpersonal skills.[15] Why? Because they're constantly doubting their worth and accomplishments. They think they're on the verge of being "found out," and they don't want to draw any negative attention, so they focus on pleasing others. The author of the study goes on to suggest a more nuanced approach to treating Imposter Syndrome based on the perceived positive effects that accompany the negative. That's the thing—the negatives are still there. While increased interpersonal effectiveness is great, it comes at the massive cost of all the negative symptoms that accompany it.

Essentially, the research didn't tell us anything we (experts) didn't already know: individuals with Imposter Syndrome are hardworking, high-performing, and often have strong interpersonal skills. None of this negates the mental, physical, and emotional harm that prolonged Imposter thoughts, feelings, and behaviors can cause.

### Everyone experiences Imposter Syndrome.

The generalization that "we all have it" minimizes the experiences of those genuinely struggling. While research suggests that up to 70 percent of people may encounter Imposter Syndrome, it's imperative not to dilute its gravity or assign labels, stereotypes, or other "descriptions" of what people with Imposter Syndrome look like or have been through. We don't put people in a box.

I speak to individuals regularly who do not and never have experienced Imposter Syndrome. These individuals carry professional titles such as neuroscientist, marketing director, CEO, board member, head of HR, management consultant, brand manager, entrepreneur, professional athlete, and surgeon. They're all high achievers, but Imposter Syndrome isn't a part of their experience. I call this "the Oprah effect." Why? Because despite having all the background and environmental exposures that are common with Imposter Syndrome, Oprah has never experienced it. She always believed she was destined for greatness.

As she says, "I don't have any of those imposter feelings that so many people have." She goes on to explain, "I don't have high highs and I don't have low lows. Which is a good thing, because no matter what I'm going through, I know I'm going to come out of it, and be okay."[16]

Her words intersect beautifully with Imposter Syndrome. It's not your fault that you're dealing with Imposter Syndrome, but the good news is, you hold the power to conquer it.

**Confident people don't experience Imposter Syndrome.**

Imposter Syndrome isn't about a lack of confidence. One can be outwardly confident, even the most vivacious in a room, and still internally grapple with feelings of unworthiness. I know this personally and professionally, having coached many highly confident individuals. I also had high confidence, but that didn't stop my Imposter Syndrome from emerging. The phenomenon is linked more to self-worth than self-confidence.

### Imposter Syndrome keeps you humble.

Humility shouldn't stem from holding yourself back from acknowledging your hard work and success. Authentic humility doesn't have its roots in self-devaluation or attributing your talent, intelligence, qualifications, and success to constantly feeling like you're being exposed as a fraud. You don't need to hold on to Imposter Syndrome to stay humble. In fact, it will keep you in a self-deprecating state that has far broader implications.

### The workplace is to blame.

While toxic workplaces and negative systemic structures can exacerbate feelings associated with Imposter Syndrome, they're seldom the sole cause. The phenomenon's roots often trace back to individual pasts, notably experiences in childhood or adolescence. So, your workplace may be the trigger of your Imposter Syndrome, but it isn't necessarily the origin of your feelings. This doesn't mean workplaces don't need to change—they do. We'll be exploring this later.

**Success is the antidote for Imposter Syndrome.**

Many assume that success acts as an antidote for the feelings associated with Imposter Syndrome. However, the truth is counterintuitive. If you don't deal with the root cause of your Imposter Syndrome, success can exacerbate these feelings. You have "more to lose," and the fear of being found out can increase dramatically.

Renowned celebrities like Tina Fey, Tom Hanks, and even Maya Angelou have expressed feeling like frauds, despite their overwhelming success. Even Olympic gold medalists like Suni Lee, music stars like Harry Styles and Robbie Williams, and media hosts like the late Michael Parkinson haven't escaped the reach of Imposter Syndrome. No number of Oscars, medals, accolades, or acknowledgments can protect us. Although we can still achieve a good height of success with Imposter Syndrome, the toll on our mental health and wellbeing can be catastrophic. We can be destined to never feel "good enough," especially when success comes fast or reaches great heights. Plus, Imposter Syndrome robs you of the joy of truly celebrating your success. You never truly feel worthy or deserving while the shadow of

Imposter Syndrome looms large. Imagine winning an Oscar, a gold medal, performing in front of 100,000 people or running a successful business and feeling like a fraud.

The proliferation of such misconceptions doesn't just misinform; it also harms. When we oversimplify, generalize, or romanticize Imposter Syndrome, we risk invalidating the very real struggles of those affected. It's a call for all of us, whether we're experts, sufferers, or observers, to prioritize understanding over opinion and compassion over judgment.

Armed with awareness, empathy, and accurate information, we can work toward creating a space where those dealing with Imposter Syndrome feel seen, heard, and validated.

## THE IMPACT OF IMPOSTER SYNDROME

---

*Imposter Syndrome can be debilitating, and its impact isn't confined to your career. It can also take the lead in your personal life.*
*—Alison Shamir*

---

Imposter Syndrome doesn't just reside in the mind. Its shadow extends, affecting our mental, physical, emotional, and even financial wellbeing. In fact, research shows that worry, depression, and anxiety resulting from pressure to "live up to one's successful image and fear that one will be exposed as unworthy and incompetent" often accompany Imposter feelings.[17]

It makes sense, right? When we're constantly battling persistent self-doubt and feelings of fraudulence—despite evidence of our capabilities and accomplishments—it can erode our self-esteem, self-confidence, and diminish our already fragile sense of self-worth. Our emotional wellbeing can take a massive hit.

For those suffering, it's a vicious cycle. We tie our worth to our accomplishments yet, at the same time, discount those accomplishments. Without understanding and addressing the phenomenon and associated behavior, we struggle to pull ourselves out of that endless loop until something inside us breaks, and we, for example, break down in the office bathroom.

Imposter Syndrome, with its wide-reaching effects, is a phenomenon that demands attention, understanding, and compassionate intervention. As we delve deeper into the topic, we'll uncover its layers, understand its roots, and, most importantly, learn to navigate and conquer it. My aim is to shine a light on this shadow, making the invisible visible and handing the power back to *you*.

# CHAPTER TWO

"You are not
one-dimensional,
neither is your
Imposter Syndrome."

—Alison Shamir

# IMPOSTER ORIGINS

## WHAT'S YOUR STORY?

*It's my mother's fault.*

As heartbreaking as it was to come to that conclusion in 2014 when I was well into my breakup with Imposter Syndrome, it also gave me clarity. I could finally begin to release it. I could finally begin to heal.

When I was four years old, my mother abandoned me and our family. She wanted to divorce my father, and one day she just got up and left. She disappeared for a few months, leaving three children behind before resurfacing to serve my father with divorce papers. Thus began an awful period for our family.

We were torn apart. I was ripped from our family home despite living there with my father and two brothers and it being a short distance from my school. My mother was awarded custody. I have no idea who in the family law court thought that was a good idea, to pull apart a family and uproot a young child from everything she knew as stable and comfortable. Their ruling tipped my life upside down.

This was the beginning of a highly traumatic and abusive childhood at the hands of my mother and her new husband(s). Because of her, growing up, I never felt good enough, worthy enough, or smart enough.

I believed that if my own mother didn't love me, subjected me to abuse, and knowingly sat by while others abused me, then how worthy of anything good could I really be? Her rejection of my authentic sexuality—along with her new husband being grossly homophobic—was a severe emotional and mental blow.

I felt such significant moments of shame in what was meant to be my safe environment, my home. To cope with what had happened to me, I developed a severe eating disorder for two years in my teens—that was the beginning of my perfectionist tendencies. I tried to have the perfect teen body; I tried to take control of whatever I could.

During this teen period, I also experienced significant mental and physical trauma at the hands of one of my brothers who, in a violent rage, dived across a kitchen island bench, smashed me, including my head, into the wall oven, and tried to kill me by strangulation. Thankfully, my father was home. He saved my life. This trauma sent me into a further spin of shock, fear, and despair. I felt so alone, yet I carried on. I compartmentalized it, put on my stoic front, and continued with life, leaning further on my perfectionist tendencies for a sense of "control." In hindsight, I should have gone to therapy and sought professional help. In fact, when I think back to that pain—mental, physical, emotional—I don't know how I survived it. The perfectionist tendencies stayed with me when I entered the workforce, and they became my key sabotaging behavior driven by my Imposter Syndrome.

The only silver linings I have tried to draw from this early period of my life is that I had to be independent, resilient, and stoic, traits I've carried into adulthood that have served me well. However, I have a complicated relationship with vulnerability—something I've worked on extensively over the years and needed to if I wanted to become the type of speaker and coach I am today. At a young age, I also developed a high level of confidence because I had to fend for myself. This has also served me well. Although it didn't stop the Imposter Syndrome, it certainly helped navigate through it.

This is my origin story. *What's yours?*

## Imposter Origin Stories—Often Similar, But Never the Same

---

*"Everyone who suffers from Imposter Syndrome has an origin story. You may not know or understand yours yet, but this book will help you to unearth it and connect the dots."*
*—Alison Shamir*

---

Throughout my career, I've been entrusted with many origin stories. They span a variety of situations and environmental factors, including but not limited to:

- Harsh criticism and high expectations from parents—the individual literally being told that anything less than a perfect grade or result wasn't good enough.
- Parents or caregivers claiming credit for the individual's success, even using language like, "You only achieved this because of me."
- Beratement or humiliation from caregivers or teachers, often public and in front of peers. In one particular case, a boy being told he was "the class clown" and would never amount to anything became the seed of Imposter Syndrome.
- Being labeled the "sporty one" when in fact the individual was just as intelligent as their siblings or others.
- Friendship groups telling an individual, "You're not smart enough" to chase their dream of being a doctor, pilot, and so on.
- Discrimination based on socioeconomic status, being told, "People like you don't make it," or, "You don't fit in here."

- Attacks on personal appearance or habits, such as being told, "Stop eating so much because you'll get fat and no one will want to marry you."
- The individual knowing they were "different" or in the minority, or being told they were, whether based on gender, sexuality, disability, or neurodiversity, and often having to hide it.
- Coming from privilege and, despite working hard, the individual always believing they had an "advantage," diluting their own views of competence and worthiness. We see this often in children of very successful or famous people. They can struggle to find their own identity, and, even if they do, there are always people around them who want to connect their earned success with that of their parents. At times, it's like no matter what they do or how many paths they carve, they'll never get the credit they deserve.

Over the years, I've learned that, regardless of your past, one thing remains true: understanding your origin story brings clarity and the ability to shed the weight of self-blame—because Imposter Syndrome is not your fault.

* * *

## 360 DEGREES OF IMPOSTER SYNDROME

When I began my journey out of Imposter Syndrome, I soon realized that "positive thinking" wasn't going to cut it. I had to get to the bottom of my Imposter Syndrome, the root cause, not just the symptoms. That meant going deeper than just the mind. I needed to explore the workings of my brain. Personal study wasn't enough; I wanted to learn from the best neuroscientists. In 2021, I began to combine personal study with formal training and certifications in the field of applied neuroscience and brain health led by the wonderful Dr. Sarah McKay and her Neuroscience Academy, followed by further studies as a founding member of Sarah's Neuroscience Coaching Network, codirected by the equally wonderful Dr. Mary Collins.

Spending a great amount of time and effort on learning (which still continues today) the most recent developments in neuroscience, human behavior, and habits has ensured that my proprietary frameworks for conquering Imposter Syndrome are evidence-based and science-backed, which is why they work. Clients who have completed my Conquer Your Imposter™ coaching program, and high-performing and high-achieving individuals, have regularly described it and their results as "life-changing."

My intent with this book isn't to bury you in data. Instead, I've aimed to include a good mix of hard statistics, evidence-based information, and storytelling to best help you understand your own journey with Imposter Syndrome, feel less alone, and know how to help yourself or others.

**Imposter Syndrome is not a "one-size-fits-all experience," because you are unique, and no one has walked in your shoes.**

There are, however, some commonalities that can flow through our Imposter journeys. Before we get to those, let's first explore the brain—from the bottom up, outside in, and top down.

A useful framework created by Dr. Sarah McKay, neuroscientist and author, to conceptualize how biology, culture, and psychology interact to sculpt our brains is the Bottom-Up, Outside-In, Top-Down model. It's loosely inspired by the well-known biopsychosocial model, which considers the interactions of biological, psychological, and social factors on our health over the lifespan. Sarah's framework puts the brain in the middle.

- **Bottom-Up** elements are the biological or physiological determinants of brain health, development, and aging. Our brains receive constant streams of data about what's happening inside our bodies, some of which we're conscious of, other factors we're unaware of. Bottom-Up elements include genes, hormones, the immune system, nutrition, exercise, sleep, and other lifestyle choices.

- **Outside-In** elements are outside us and make their way in via our senses (what we see, hear, smell, touch, and taste). Outside includes our social circle, the culture we've grown up in, the built and natural environment, current circumstances, and external stressors.

- **Top-Down** elements include what we think of as our mind—our conscious thoughts, emotions, personality, language, expectations, and belief systems.

Not only do these many elements regulate the brain's development, performance, and health, but each element interacts with and influences others in dynamic ways.[1]

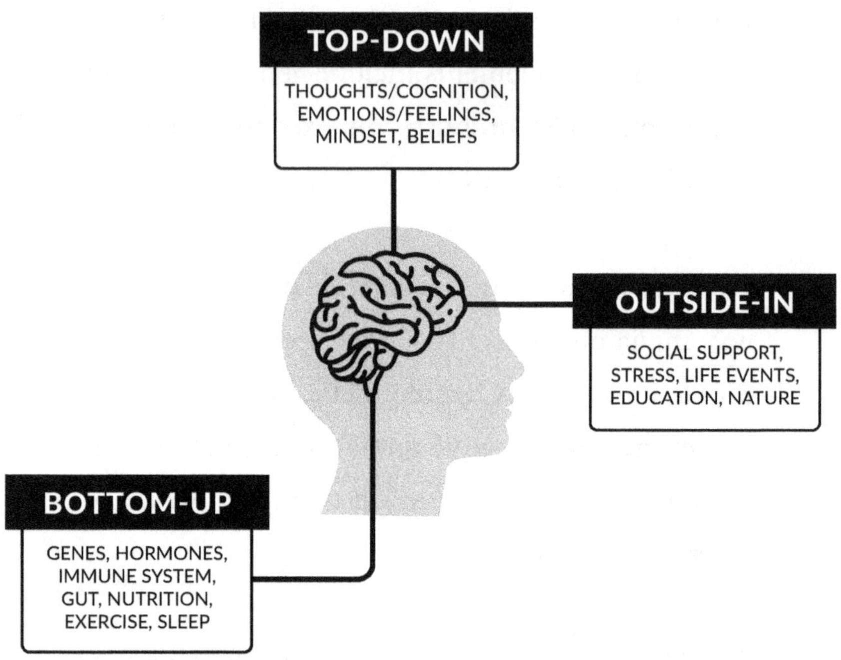


*Source:* The Women's Brain Book, *Dr. Sarah McKay.*

So much information pushed in the market and across the web focuses on "top down" factors, such as thoughts and emotions, but Imposter Syndrome is more complex and nuanced than that.

By understanding and viewing Imposter Syndrome as a 3D phenomenon, we can focus on the aspects that really matter first, as the order in which we navigate Imposter Syndrome is critical to gaining long-term control or eliminating it entirely. Either result is good because you've regained control.

# THE FOUNDATIONS OF IDENTITY AND ROOTS OF IMPOSTER SYNDROME

For many who suffer from Imposter Syndrome, the seed of "I'm not good enough" or feeling unworthy is planted in childhood. This is due to a parental, guardian, or social situation in which you were made to feel less than.

**We call this your "origin story."**

As highlighted in the examples I shared earlier, many Imposter origin stories involve harsh criticism, unrealistic expectations, discrimination, and numerous other experiences. While everyone's story is different, certain elements are often similar.

To get to the very root of Imposter Syndrome, we must understand the foundations of our identities. What is Identity? I'll give you a hint—it's not what you do for work. There's much more to it than that.

## Origins of Identity

Identity can be understood as an amalgamation of the beliefs, values, and understandings we hold about ourselves. It's our answer to the question, "Who am I?" This complex web of self-conceptions starts forming early in life and is continually evolving, influenced by both internal and external factors.

Current identity research states that our identities are largely shaped by both close and distant influences, close being family and friends and distant being society at large. Also, the better we understand who we are, the more influence we're able to exert on the world around us.[2] Essentially, the world shapes us, and, with enough personal identity awareness, we have the power to shape the world in return. It's one of many great reasons to explore exactly who you are.

Your identity forms over time, with formation beginning practically on day one.

### The Crucial Period: 0–7 Years

Between the ages of 0 and 7 years, the brain is incredibly malleable. Termed the "imprint phase," during this time, children are like sponges, absorbing information from the world around them. It's the time when our foundational beliefs, behaviors, and values start taking shape. It is also during this period that the seeds of Imposter Syndrome can be sown.

From 0 to 2 years, attachment and trust are key. Infants depend on caregivers for everything, and how these caregivers respond to the child's needs plays a crucial role in shaping their identity. Consistent care helps cultivate a sense of security, while inconsistent or negligent care can lead to feelings of worthlessness.

From 2 to 7 years, as the child grows and begins to interact more with the outside world, they're learning societal norms and values. They're watching, imitating, and listening. Feedback from parents, teachers, and peers is internalized and plays a significant role in self-worth. This is the phase where notions of success and failure, right and wrong, and self-worth begin to solidify. It was during this period that my parents divorced and the subsequent experiences turned my life upside down.

## Factors That Shape Identity

As we develop, several critical factors work together to shape our identities.

> **Parental influence.** A parent's beliefs, values, behaviors, and feedback play a paramount role in the development of a child's identity. Praise can cultivate confidence, while excessive criticism can lead to feelings of unworthiness and self-doubt.

> **Cultural and social conditioning.** The culture we're born into provides a set of norms, values, and beliefs. Societal expectations about gender roles, success, appearance, and so on can exert enormous

pressure on individuals, steering them away from their authentic selves.

**Experiences.** Events in early life, such as successes, failures, traumas, and critical incidents, are deeply internalized and can become a fixed part of our identities. For example, a child constantly ridiculed for their efforts might grow up believing they can never be good enough.

**Peer influence.** The desire to fit in can lead children to mold their behaviors, values, and beliefs in alignment with their peer group. This can sometimes mean suppressing their true selves.

Identity isn't static. It can, and often does, evolve as we evolve. Shifts in identity can come through age, growth, relationships, and other factors, and when our identity is changing or being compromised, it can leave us feeling shaky. The key is to tune in, listen, and try to understand what's happening. Otherwise, Imposter feelings can emerge.

# IT'S NOT YOUR FAULT—DIGGING TO THE ROOTS

When we dig to the roots of Imposter Syndrome, what can we expect to find?

Just like identity, Imposter Syndrome can stem from a combination of psychological, environmental, social, and cultural factors. While everyone's experience is different, there are some common reasons why we may experience the phenomenon.

## Early Life Experiences

As mentioned, early experiences, family dynamics, and upbringing play a big part in shaping our identities.

In her 1990 dissertation, Camille Bussotti suggested that, in families in which support for a child's feelings and individual development was lacking, the child who becomes an "Imposter" may have experienced parentification (taking on adult responsibilities) or in some other way been required to develop a "false self" in order to receive validation. This false self is likely to then carry into adulthood, presenting as insecurity about their true identity and often playing out as Imposter feelings in those who are successful.[3]

Other childhood experiences, such as receiving excessive praise or criticism for achievements, can also shape an individual's self-perception and contribute to Imposter Syndrome. For example, if we're constantly told we are "special" or "gifted," we may develop a fear of not living up to those expectations and worry that we'll be exposed as less competent than others believe. Further, if the expectation of us is "it's A-plus or nothing," it can create early perfectionist tendencies that carry through into adulthood. Pressure and labels from parents, caregivers, or teachers can force a child to push beyond their natural abilities out of fear of causing disappointment. Similarly, comparison with siblings, especially high achievers, carries weight and can lead to pressure to perform to the same high standard.

### Pressure to Represent Groups or Cultures

Pressure to represent groups or cultures can also be a catalyst for Imposter Syndrome. The experience of American gymnast and Olympic gold medalist Suni Lee is a prime example.

When she competed in the 2020 Tokyo Olympic Games, Lee made history by becoming the first Hmong American to compete for Team USA and also the first to win an Olympic gold medal. The pressure to represent her culture was immense, which led to anxiety and Imposter Syndrome.

In an interview with ESPN, Lee said, "I feel like after the Olympics, there's just been so much doubt in like, 'Oh, she shouldn't have won Olympics, blah, blah, blah,' and it really hits my soul ... I think I just put in my head that I didn't deserve to win ... Like, impostor syndrome ... That's exactly what I have."[4]

Even though she had achieved the ultimate success in her chosen sport—winning a gold medal at the Olympics—Lee still felt like an Imposter. Sound familiar? As we know, success isn't the cure for Imposter Syndrome. Instead, we must address the root cause.

In Lee's case, the pressure came from many angles. Not only was she performing for herself but also for her family, community, and country. For her, the stakes were high. As her father, John Lee, said before the all-around Olympic gymnastics final, "As I watch her I'll be thinking, 'If she brings home a couple of medals, hopefully, a couple of gold, I mean, that would be so great for the family, the community, and for the USA."[5]

For Suni Lee, the pressure to perform for the groups she represented was real.

Discussing representing her school, she said, "When everybody expects you to be good for Auburn, it's really hard for me just mentally, because I already put so much pressure on myself that when I have that extra pressure stress added on to it, I just kind of break."[6]

Pressure to perform can come from many sources. In Lee's case, as is the case with many high performers, she was forced to deal with those pressures at a very young age. She was just eighteen years old when she represented her community and country on the world stage. For Suni Lee, the conditions for Imposter Syndrome to grow and take hold were ideal.

## Socioeconomic Status

Socioeconomic status is another factor that can lead to Imposter Syndrome. Those who grow up underprivileged can feel "less than," especially when stepping into environments that are far removed from what they're used to, for example, when transitioning from high school to university or entering the workforce. They may have grown up in a working-class family and perhaps even experienced poverty, affording them fewer opportunities than those who were more well-off. When they move into new environments, they perform social comparison with the people around them, believing others to be more talented, competent, or successful due to their backgrounds, consequently leading to feelings of inadequacy. Even when they're at the same school or in the same office as everyone else, even when they've proven themselves and earned the right to be there, they still feel like they don't belong. They feel like frauds.

When someone with a poor socioeconomic background becomes wildly successful, the Imposter Syndrome can magnify, which is something English media host and journalist Michael Parkinson experienced. Parkinson grew up in public housing and had to work his way out of poverty. Even though he regularly interviewed some of the biggest celebrities in the world, he suffered from insecurity, self-doubt, and, as a result, Imposter Syndrome. Due to his background, he constantly questioned his success, as did some of the leaders at the BBC where he worked.[7] Who was he, some poor kid from South Yorkshire whose father was a coal miner, to be sitting across from all those big names? We don't easily forget where we came from, and sometimes neither do the people around us, which can create fertile ground for Imposter Syndrome.

Michael Parkinson's story is especially illuminating because it proves the idea that success isn't a cure for Imposter Syndrome. If it were, Parkinson, after reaching the pinnacle of success in his industry, wouldn't have felt the way he did. However, he lived under the shadow of Imposter Syndrome for his entire career.

Additionally, affirmative action for BIPOC (black, indigenous, and people of color) in the United States can further fuel socioeconomic-status-related Imposter Syndrome. In short, affirmative action is a DEI (diversity, equity, and inclusion) measure that aims to create equal opportunities for underrepresented and disadvantaged groups. It has, at times, been seen as a controversial approach that some label unfair and even damaging to those it aims to help.[8] While, for some, receiving a scholarship or similar is a huge and wonderful opportunity, one they grab on to and build upon as a strong foundation for ongoing success, for others, it can lead them to think that without it they never would have made it and therefore aren't good enough. This is exacerbated if they step into environments where they're made to feel less than by peers. In such cases, Imposter thoughts can emerge.

### Stereotype Threat

For individuals belonging to underrepresented groups or facing stereotypes, Imposter Syndrome can be amplified. The cause? Something called stereotype threat.

According to social psychologists Claude Steele and Joshua Aronson, stereotype threat is "being at risk of confirming, as self-characteristic, a negative stereotype about one's group."[9]

In relation to Imposter Syndrome, the pressure to disprove stereotypes or meet higher expectations can intensify feelings of inadequacy and the fear of being perceived as not good enough or a fraud, particularly in academic and professional settings.

### Example of Stereotype Threat: Gender and Math Performance

A 1999 study demonstrated that when women were reminded of the stereotype that "men are better at math," their performance on a challenging math test declined compared to men. However, when the same test was described without mentioning the stereotype, women performed just as well as men.[10] This finding highlights how stereotype threat can undermine the abilities of individuals in high-stakes situations.

### Compromised Sense of Self-Worth and Identity

Trauma, abuse, neglect, rejection, and other experiences that compromise our sense of self-worth and identity can lead to Imposter Syndrome.

My own origin story demonstrates this point, as the trauma and abuse I suffered as a child were the seeds of my Imposter Syndrome. Growing up, I never felt good enough, and those feelings carried through to my adult life, causing me to question every success along the way. However, once I identified the root cause, I was able to start the healing process and lean into my authentic self. Getting to the root cause is vital.

## THE DRIFT FROM AUTHENTICITY TO FEELING LIKE AN IMPOSTER

When there's a dissonance between our true self (who we are at our core) and the identities we've been conditioned to adopt, the feeling of being an Imposter can arise. As we navigate the complexities of life, we can often wear masks to fit in, to meet expectations, or to protect ourselves. Over time, the line between the mask and the self can become blurred. We lose ourselves and tie our identities to our achievements, which increases symptoms of Imposter Syndrome.

---

*"Even when a mask fits well—even looks good on a person—there comes a time when that mask grows heavy, uncomfortable, and probably suffocating. Sooner or later, the mask needs to come off."*[11]
*—Dr. Pauline Rose Clance*

---

Adulthood is when we typically see Imposter Syndrome raise its head.

Symptoms can manifest in several ways:

- Fear of being exposed as an intellectual fraud despite your accomplishments (the hallmark of Imposter Syndrome).

- Chronic doubt about your own skills, talents, and abilities despite evidence of your competence.
- Not believing you're worthy of current or future opportunities.
- Attributing success to external factors, like luck, charm, or third parties. I call this the "luck default."
- Inability to accept praise and deflecting compliments about yourself and your achievements.
- Perfectionist tendencies like setting unrealistic expectations on yourself, harsh self-criticism, and never being satisfied (even if you do produce a good result).
- Excessive fear of failure, mistakes, and criticism, which leads to catastrophic thinking.
- Fear and guilt around success.
- Constant need for external validation and approval or to "be the best."
- Not feeling good enough or worthy of love in personal relationships, leading to feeling like you have to hide your true self.

In their 1985 book, Joan C. Harvey and Cynthia Katz defined the three stand-out components of Imposter Syndrome:

1. The belief that you have fooled others.
2. Fear of being exposed as an imposter.

3. Inability to attribute your achievements to personal qualities such as ability, intelligence, and skills.[12]

These components can play out significantly in our careers. But it's important to note …

**You are more than your achievements.**

While your accomplishments shape your journey, they don't define your self-worth. When working to overcome Imposter Syndrome, it's crucial to separate yourself from the external validation of achievements and learn to stand firmly in your inherent value. This can only come from within, and the beauty is, it's 100 percent within your control.

Your career may change (and often does), and tying your identity to work and work alone or your performance—referred to as performance-based identity—can leave your foundations fragile when even minor changes take place. Your accomplishments are the cherry on top. They don't define you. You define you. The key is to tie identity to purpose and worth, not performance.

No matter how Imposter Syndrome shows itself for you, all imposter roads lead to shame, fear of being found out or exposed, and assuming a persona, mask, or set of actions to hide your perceived inadequacies, which feel very real. This is the power Imposter Syndrome can have over us.

Understanding the origins of your identity and the factors that influence it can empower you to reclaim your authenticity. While societal pressures and early conditioning play a role, it's crucial to recognize that identity is fluid. With introspection, awareness, and support, you can peel back the layers, address the roots of Imposter Syndrome, and step confidently into your true self.

In subsequent chapters, we'll delve deeper into strategies and interventions that you can employ to conquer Imposter Syndrome, helping you lead a life that resonates with your authentic self while taking into account the evolution of your identity as you grow and experience life.

As you begin to unravel your own Imposter origin story, it can help to hear the stories of others. Remember, you're not alone.

## ORIGIN STORY CASE STUDY: TERRI

*Terri is a business leader, who, like many of us, can trace her Imposter Syndrome back to her childhood. Her story may help you understand yours.*

> I've always been a very sensitive person. Even as a child, I was incredibly empathetic, which is a great quality, but it can have its downsides,

especially considering how my childhood ended up playing out.

Growing up, my family moved around a lot. My parents ran hotels, and each year we would arrive at a new place where we'd run and fix up a hotel before moving on to the next. New town, new hotel, new school, new friends—every year. I was always the new girl, and although I got very good at fitting in, I never quite felt like I belonged. But constantly moving around wasn't the worst part of my childhood.

When I was ten years old, my father died by suicide. It was a double whammy of grief. I wasn't just dealing with the grief of loss but also the grief caused by the choice my father made. I couldn't help but question my self-worth. *Why would he do this? Why couldn't he stay? Wasn't I good enough?* The grief and insecurity became deeply set in my psyche.

Before my father died, we moved to a new suburb, and left a low socioeconomic area, to live in an affluent area. At my previous school, I was top of the class and became vice captain. Naturally, I began to develop a sense that I was capable and smart. My self-esteem was at an all-time high.

However, when we moved, suddenly I wasn't at the top of the class anymore. The bar was much higher, which shows the difference between low and high socioeconomic areas, and I no longer felt capable or smart. I recall one embarrassing moment where I couldn't answer a specific question in class, and I felt stupid. I didn't feel like I fit in at all. All that self-esteem I had built up at my previous school got knocked right back down.

When my father died, I experienced a lot of shame. No one else's father had died. No one else was without a father. No one's parents were even divorced. Among my classmates, I was the odd one out, and fitting in seemed impossible. This, along with continually being the new girl, set me up to experience Imposter Syndrome later in life.

As it turned out, I wasn't stupid after all; I went on to do OK at school and got into a business degree at university. Once I completed my degree, I moved to Sydney with no job and nowhere to live, throwing myself into a new and uncertain situation and making it all work.

My first job was at a marketing agency, which put me on a career trajectory of working in and around creativity, which I came to love. At one point, I was working in an agency as a senior account director, and I was overseeing the team that managed our clients and projects. The agency didn't have a general manager, even though it was clear to me we needed one. I entertained the idea that I could do the job, but I would need to convince my boss. *What am I doing?* I thought. *I can't be a general manager. What was I thinking?* I didn't feel worthy of the position—the story of my life at that point—so I abandoned the idea … until the people who loved me changed my mind.

Fortunately for me, others believed in me. They offered me nothing but encouragement, and their support made me stop and reconsider. *What's stopping me? What's the worst that could happen? At the very worst, my boss could say "no," and that's it. I really have nothing to lose.*

Personally, I visualize Imposter Syndrome as someone having a rope tied around my waist, and every time I try to move forward, they pull me right back. It's a protection mechanism driven by fear, trying to prevent me from getting hurt, even when I don't need protection.

But with the support of loved ones, I prepared a presentation and delivered my pitch to my boss. I basically told her, "This is what you need. This is why you need it. And this is why it should be me."

Her response? "OK."

OK. Just like that. What was I even worried about?

If I hadn't been able to reframe my thinking, I would have missed out on the opportunity. I was still thinking like the confused ten-year-old who was used to sabotaging herself. I wasn't her anymore, but I needed a circuit breaker, some supportive voices to break the pattern and help me see myself and the situation clearly.

Once I was in the role, I decided I needed some additional support in the form of coaching or mentoring, but I didn't know where to turn. Serendipitously, someone I worked with had just completed a marketing program. Essentially, it was nine months of coaching, mentoring, and learning. But there was a catch: the program only accepted thirty people at a time, and there was a strict application process.

Once again, that voice set in. *Why even apply? I'll never get in. Why would they want me?* And once again, I realized I was repeating the same old pattern, the one I had already proven to be wrong when I got the general manager position.

When I applied to the program, which involved submitting a video application, I was up against 400 other applications. It was daunting—but I got in, joining twenty-nine other successful applicants in the program.

I've learned that if you can't be your own circuit breaker, you need someone to be it for you. Nowadays, when I catch myself slipping into those old patterns of self-sabotage, I'm usually able to redirect the story I tell myself and my own thoughts. For years, however, I needed someone else to be the voice of reason, but it's important that I'm now that person for myself.

Honestly, I still sometimes struggle with how I perceive myself, and I need to remind myself of everything I've achieved. If you also struggle with self-perception, the Johari Window is a great tool for helping you see yourself how others see you. Essentially, you choose five or six positive words from a list that you think describe you. Then you send the test to others who know you well so they can do the same, choosing words they think describe you. You then receive the results with

| | Known to self | Not known to self |
|---|---|---|
| Known to others | OPEN AREA | BLIND SPOT |
| Not known to others | HIDDEN AREA | UNKNOWN |

*The Johari Window Model*

words categorized as **open** (known to you and others), **blind** (known to others but not you), and **hidden** (known to you but not others).

When I compared the words I used to describe myself with the words others used, I noticed that my language was a lot softer, for example, caring, kind, warm, whereas others used stronger words, such as confident, powerful, brave, intelligent, independent, trustworthy, witty. *Whoa, hang on a sec … people see me as a lot stronger than I see myself.* It was a total revelation. *I must be doing something right. The way I'm presenting myself must be right, and now I just need to ride the wave and stop doubting myself. I've got this.*

I spent a lifetime trying to prove myself, and it wasn't until my late forties that I changed the story

I tell myself from *I'm not good enough* to *I'm a very capable person*. After all the years of self-doubt and feeling like an Imposter, I can finally reflect on my achievements and see myself how others see me—smart, powerful, capable.

Now, when I want something, I don't let the rope around my waist pull me back. Instead, I just go for it. I mean, what's the worst that could happen?

## WHAT YOU BELIEVE IS WHO YOU BECOME

---

*"The gap between feeling like an Imposter and not feeling like an Imposter is not bridged by action; it is bridged by belief in yourself. The action is secondary."*
*—Alison Shamir*

---

In this chapter, we've discussed how multiple factors make up your Imposter experience. Imposter Syndrome is a complex and multifaceted phenomenon, and different people experience it for different reasons—we're all unique. However, belief is always a big part of the cause and the solution.

One group of psychiatric researchers provides an excellent description of how beliefs function:

> Beliefs originate from what we hear—and keep on hearing from others, ever since we were children (and even before that!). The sources of beliefs include environment, events, knowledge, past experiences, visualisation etc. One of the biggest misconceptions people often harbour is that belief is a static, intellectual concept. Nothing can be farther from truth. Beliefs are a choice. We have the power to choose our beliefs and our beliefs become our reality.[13]

At its core, Imposter Syndrome is tied to your belief system. You have the talent, intelligence, qualifications, and accomplishments, but you don't believe you're deserving. You believe you're fooling everyone or have fluked your way to where you are now. The key to dismantling Imposter Syndrome is to attack it at its foundations. Gradually, its hold on you will weaken. In the end, it will come crashing down, and you will take control. However, before we can conquer the Imposter, we must understand where it comes from.

In this sense, understanding our limiting beliefs is a critical part of conquering Imposter Syndrome. Essentially, limiting beliefs are invisible barriers, self-imposed restrictions that hinder us from realizing our full potential. These beliefs convince us we're inadequate, powerless, or fundamentally lacking in some way. Be it about our intelligence, appearance, capabilities, or worthiness, these beliefs subtly thread through our thoughts and decisions, often unchallenged and unverified.

Take, for example, a person who consistently delivers exceptional work but dismisses compliments, attributing their success to luck or other external factors. This is more than modesty; it's a reflection of a deep-seated belief: "I'm not competent enough, and someday others will see it." This is a classic case of Imposter Syndrome anchored by a limiting belief.

The key to understanding Imposter Syndrome and our "origin story" is that moment or series of moments in our past that scripted our limiting beliefs: the unkind word from a teacher, a parent's high expectations, bullying from peers, racism, or discrimination from society. Such instances sculpt our internal narrative about our own worth and capabilities. These stories, once told often enough, become internalized to the point where they're accepted as truth, consequently shaping our actions and reactions in adulthood.

It's also imperative to differentiate between beliefs, thoughts, and feelings, even though they're intricately interwoven. Our belief systems, when dominated by limiting beliefs, generate repetitive negative thoughts that stir corresponding feelings. For instance, a belief such as *I'm not good enough* produces thoughts like *I won't be able to do this*, leading to feelings of anxiety or inadequacy. Therefore, in order to dismantle Imposter Syndrome, we start with the belief.

These limiting beliefs feed the Imposter Syndrome, providing a continual source of self-doubt and fear of exposure, despite evidence to prove we belong where we are. When we succeed, these beliefs tell us it's a fluke. When we fail, they assure us our fraudulence has been unveiled.

---

*"The stories we tell ourselves around what we are exposed to in our lives create the beliefs we form. If negative, these stories and beliefs rule our lives, and we are destined to feel unworthy or like Imposters."*
*—Alison Shamir*

---

Limiting beliefs are perpetuated and intensified by stories—both the ones told to us and the narratives we tell ourselves. If a child is consistently labeled as the "slow learner," they may carry this story into adulthood, applying it even in areas where they excel, purely because it has become their internal narrative.

Here are some examples of stories you may have been exposed to that fuel a limiting belief that drives your Imposter Syndrome:

## Stories and Beliefs

| Negative Stories You May Have Been Exposed To | | Self-Limiting Beliefs That Can Form From These Stories |
|---|---|---|
| Your parent abandoned you. | → | *I'm not worthy of love.* |
| Children/women should be seen and not heard. | → | *My voice has no value.* |
| Nobody likes a show-off. | → | *Celebrating my good work or achievements makes me look bad.* |
| People like us don't go to university. | → | *I'm not good enough to go to university.* |
| When you grow up, the only careers you should consider are these ones … | → | *If I don't secure a certain career, I'm a failure.* |
| You're the sporty one, not the smart one. | → | *I'm not intelligent enough.* |
| If you don't get it perfect, don't even bother. | → | *Only perfect is good enough.* |
| There's no point even trying. You'll never be as good as that other person. | → | *I am inferior.* |

Each time the narrative is validated, even in the smallest of ways, it solidifies the limiting belief. Individuals wrestling with Imposter Syndrome see a missed promotion or constructive criticism, while ordinary career occurrences, as proof of their Imposter status. They frequently assume the worst.

The journey toward dismantling Imposter Syndrome begins with recognizing and understanding the limiting beliefs that fuel it. It's about going back, discovering your origin story, and acknowledging its impact without surrendering to it.

# CHAPTER THREE

"You can be the most confident person in the room and still experience Imposter Syndrome."

—Alison Shamir

# TRILOGY OF SELFS

## YOUR THREE SELFS

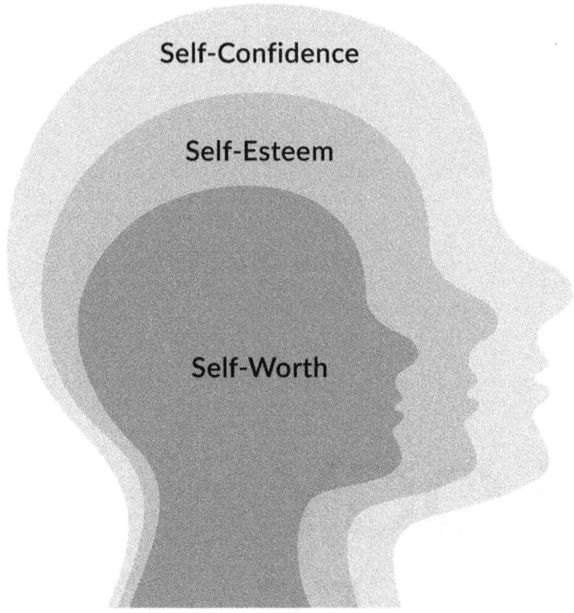


On the surface, it may seem that Imposter Syndrome is primarily linked to self-confidence. If someone is exuding confidence, there's no way they could feel like an Imposter, right? As my own experience demonstrates, it's not that simple. While I had plenty of confidence, I still felt like a fraud. Self-confidence isn't the critical component. Those who experience Imposter Syndrome are more likely to be suffering from a lack of self-worth.

However, in reality, three distinct yet interlinked selfs—self-worth, self-esteem, and self-confidence—can work together to fuel our Imposter experience. Therefore, on the road to overcoming Imposter Syndrome, it's essential that we understand these three selfs and learn to monitor them along the way.

## Defining Self-Worth, Self-Esteem, and Self-Confidence

In the grand story of personal development, confidence often takes center stage, basking in the limelight like the popular protagonist in a high school drama. It's flashy, visible, and garners applause. It opens doors, builds relationships, and helps us maintain momentum. But lurking in the background, often overlooked yet undeniably pivotal, is self-worth.

Self-worth is the quiet, profound force that truly holds the story together. Unlike its showier counterpart, it doesn't need external validation or achievements. It's that deep, internal anchor, rooted in your belief system. Confidence might be the character that turns heads, but self-worth is the scriptwriter, crafting the underlying narrative that determines the play's outcome. It's self-worth that whispers the truths about who we are at our core, beyond the accolades and achievements.

In a world that often confuses loudness with confidence, self-worth doesn't clamor for attention. But make no mistake—it's the strongest and most important pillar in the overall construction of your self. It's the unsung hero, the steady, guiding force that shapes your journey, ensuring that when you reach your destination, you truly believe you belong there.

When your self-worth is solid, you can strip away all of your achievements and still feel centered and, importantly, happy. It's that powerful.

Self-worth, self-esteem, self-confidence—while these terms are often used interchangeably, they each have unique nuances and dimensions that we'll now explore in depth.

**Self-worth** refers to the intrinsic belief and understanding that you are valuable and worthy of respect, regardless of your accomplishments, failures, or the perceptions of others. It is based on an internal recognition of your own value and remains stable and unconditional despite external circumstances. Self-worth influences how you view yourself at a foundational level. A person with high self-worth believes they deserve love, respect, and positive outcomes, irrespective of their achievements or external validations. A person with high self-worth is less likely to experience Imposter Syndrome because they can connect with and stand as their authentic self. Also important to note, you can experience low self-worth but not experience Imposter Syndrome, they can exist independently.

---

*"In life, you don't soar to the level of your hopes and dreams, you stay stuck at the level of your self-worth."*
*—Jamie Kern Lima*

---

**Self-esteem** is your overall opinion of yourself, encompassing judgments and evaluations, and is based on how you believe others perceive you. It can be influenced by external conditions, achievements, and validations, and it may involve comparing yourself to others. Self-esteem can fluctuate based on successes, failures, and feedback. High self-esteem implies a favorable view of your abilities. It enables you to approach tasks and social interactions with a positive mindset, although it may be prone to fluctuation due to its susceptibility to external factors.

**Self-confidence** is your belief in your abilities to perform tasks, navigate situations, and solve problems but is only cemented when you take action. It relates to your trust in your skills and competencies. It can be built through positive experiences and successes but also through taking difficult actions that may or may not work or get a result. Confidence is about doing. It's not about outcome, as confidence can grow from both perceived positive and negative outcomes. However, the greater your confidence, the more it influences your willingness to attempt new things and step outside of your comfort zone.

High self-confidence allows you to approach challenges with a belief that you can navigate through them successfully. It encourages risk-taking and stepping into unfamiliar territories, driving personal and professional growth. High confidence doesn't stop Imposter Syndrome surfacing, but it does help in navigating it. That's because Imposter Syndrome isn't about what you can do. Most people with Imposter Syndrome are highly skilled, intelligent, capable, competent—they're just not internalizing their achievements and success. They're still battling an underlying belief that they're not good enough.

## Interlinking Self-Worth, Self-Esteem, and Self-Confidence

Understanding the distinctions between self-worth, self-esteem, and self-confidence and how they're interrelated provides a framework to explore and address issues related to self-perception, such as Imposter Syndrome, from a multifaceted angle. The aim is to take a comprehensive approach to bolstering your self-view and tackling the challenges that arise from Imposter thoughts and feelings.

Although distinct, the three aspects of self are closely linked.

> **Self-worth as the foundation.** Self-worth provides a stable foundation. When we fundamentally believe in our inherent value, it buffers against the fluctuations in self-esteem and self-confidence that can arise due to external factors.

**Self-esteem and external influences.** While self-worth remains deeply rooted and stable, self-esteem can be swayed by external validations, achievements, and social comparisons, impacting how positively or negatively we view ourselves.

**Self-confidence and ability belief.** With a robust belief in our own worth (self-worth) and a positive evaluation of ourselves (self-esteem), confidence in our abilities (self-confidence) is likely to be strengthened, enabling the undertaking of challenges with a belief in successful outcomes and the ability to process unfavorable outcomes without harsh self-criticism.

As you seek to bolster the three aspects of self, it's important to understand that each one has a contrasting counterpart, a sinister flip side that, when you allow yourself to tilt too far in that direction, can create fertile ground for Imposter Syndrome to sprout and flourish.

Before you go any further, I have a question for you. **Who are you, really?**

I know you're a high achiever, but it's time to get more personal, to turn the focus to understanding your authentic self.

"Authentic self" refers to the core essence of who we truly are, untouched by societal expectations, judgments, or fears. It encompasses our innate desires, values, strengths, and vulnerabilities—all the components that make us uniquely individual—regardless of gender. Your authentic self is anchored in your self-worth. It's the view you have of yourself, without being tied to your achievements, work titles, or what others think of you. It's what you think of yourself and how you would describe yourself without referencing work achievements, titles, or the opinions or feedback of others.

Still with me? You might be thinking, *Why is this important?* Because operating from a place of authenticity is paramount in combating the fears and doubts fueled by Imposter Syndrome. When we're true to ourselves, we build a reservoir of self-awareness and self-trust, two other important "selfs." This foundation enables us to challenge and dissect the distorted beliefs and narratives that feed our feelings of intellectual fraudulence. When we anchor ourselves in authenticity, we not only unmask the illusions imposed by Imposter Syndrome but also build our resilience against future Imposter moments, empowering us to live and work with true confidence and purpose, being both authentic and our definition of appropriate in all situations.

So, before you go any further, I want you to answer an important question. Hint—most people find this challenging, especially their first draft. So, here's the question …

**How would you describe your own worth and value as a person, independent of your achievements, roles, or what others think of you?**

Your answer can be as long or as short as you like, as long as you feel you've answered the question.

If you need some guidance, here's an example answer (please note—job titles, achievements, or others' opinions aren't mentioned):

> *I find joy in the simple, free moments of life—the sun on my face, smelling the flowers, and swimming in the ocean, appreciating each one with gratitude. I walk through life with honesty and integrity, trusting my gut. I am decisive; I am strong, and I am resilient—I know what I want. I am both very shy but also very confident. I balance them both. I allow myself to think and grow at my own pace, but I'm not afraid to ask for help. If something feels off, I don't ignore it. I accept that life is fragile, so I live with an abundance mindset. I prioritize what brings me joy, starting with the simple things mentioned here. I fill my own cup first, so then I can always be the best version of myself.*

## THE DELICATE BALANCE BETWEEN CONFIDENCE AND SELF-DOUBT

Confidence and self-doubt are two sides of the same coin or pendulum, a delicate balance that we all navigate in our daily lives. Even though I steer away from "all or nothing" thinking, the reality is we all experience moments of doubt, just as those grappling with uncertainty can find glimpses of confidence. However, the scales can easily tip when fears like Imposter Syndrome enter the picture.

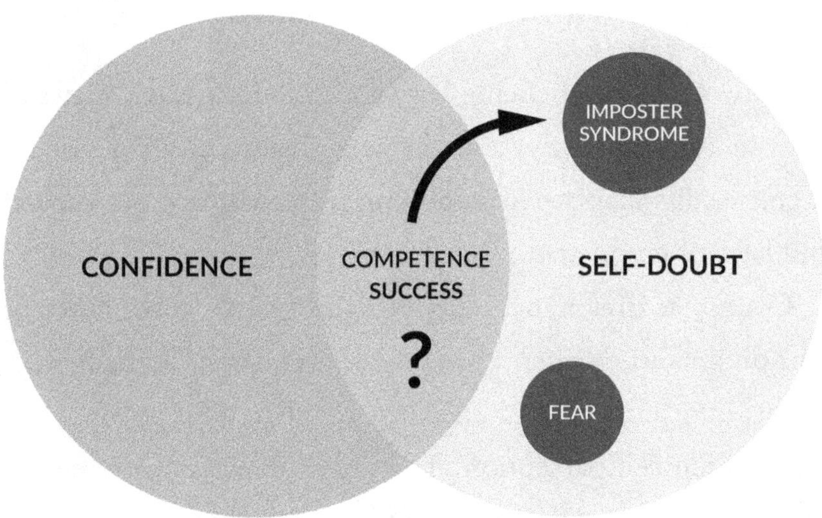


*The intersection of confidence and self-doubt.*

As we strive for balance, key questions begin to emerge:

- What does it mean to be competent?
- How do we define success?

Competence refers to the ability to do something successfully or efficiently. It encompasses having the necessary knowledge, skills, and abilities to perform a task to a satisfactory or expert level. Competence involves both the technical know-how and the application of relevant skills in practical situations, often measured against specific standards or expectations. It can also extend to emotional and interpersonal skills, particularly in leadership or collaborative roles where communication, decision-making, and problem-solving abilities are vital aspects of competence.

Now, when experiencing Imposter Syndrome, our views of both success and competence become distorted. We develop a cognitive dissonance when defining and measuring our success and level of competence.

**Cognitive dissonance** refers to the mental discomfort or tension that arises when a person holds two conflicting beliefs, values, or attitudes simultaneously, or when their actions contradict their self-perception. This psychological phenomenon often compels individuals to reduce the inconsistency and restore mental balance by altering their beliefs, attitudes, or behaviors.[1]

Imposter Syndrome, particularly in high-performing individuals, is a powerful example of cognitive dissonance in action. Here's how it works:

1. **Conflicting beliefs.** You have tangible evidence of success—awards, promotions, recognition—contrasting sharply with the internalized belief that you're not genuinely competent or deserving.

2. **Self-perception vs. reality.** Despite your accomplishments, you may attribute your success to external factors, like luck, timing, or others' generosity, rather than your own talent or hard work. This creates a dissonance between the external reality of success and your internal narrative of inadequacy.

3. **Emotional tension.** This misalignment fuels anxiety, fear of exposure as a fraud, and persistent self-doubt as the mind struggles to reconcile these opposing views.

For high-performing individuals, the stakes are particularly high because their achievements are often public and scrutinized. Addressing this cognitive dissonance is a key part of overcoming Imposter Syndrome, requiring you to remove the limiting beliefs and rewrite the story you tell yourself so you can align your self-perception with your objective success.

Questions around success and competence don't just linger in the background; they actively shape our self-perception. This is where the subtle yet powerful influence of Imposter Syndrome takes hold, skewing our views and perceptions.

High performers with Imposter Syndrome relentlessly drive themselves to unrealistically high standards of competence and success. Sound familiar? I've certainly been there, and I know that countless others have too. When Imposter thoughts take hold, our expectations of ourselves can become so high that we can never meet them. When we do deliver a "strong result," we tend to simply discount it. We're never satisfied, no matter what we achieve. When we continue to question our competence or define success through an unforgiving lens, we effectively don the "Imposter Mask," a term first coined by Dr. Pauline Clance in her groundbreaking 1985 book *The Impostor Phenomenon,* or, as I like to say, we put on "Imposter Goggles."[2] These metaphors represent how our views on competence, failure, and mistakes can distort reality.

Someone without Imposter Syndrome might view a mistake as a learning opportunity, a natural part of growth. It comes down to the story they tell themself. In contrast, someone with Imposter Syndrome will see the same mistake as a glaring confirmation of their inadequacy. Even the most minute mistake can be catastrophic to someone with Imposter Syndrome. The distinct difference isn't rooted in our level of confidence, but in how we perceive and interpret our experiences. When such skewed views take over, we filter everything through a lens of self-doubt and self-criticism, convincing ourselves that we're frauds despite our achievements. Confidence isn't what differentiates those of us who struggle with Imposter Syndrome from those who don't; it's the rigid, often harsh, criteria we set for ourselves regarding what it means to be truly successful and competent.

It's imperative to remember that the dismantling of Imposter Syndrome through the enhancement of self-worth isn't a singular event but a continual process. A process where we consistently challenge, rewrite, and reaffirm our beliefs in ourselves and our abilities, ensuring that our actions are reflections not of internalized doubt, but of acknowledged and celebrated competence and worthiness. Striving for success should be driven by healthy ambition and motivation, NOT FEAR. And achieving success should bring acceptance and joy, NOT FEAR of being "found out" or losing it all.

Before we move forward, I encourage you to answer these five important questions:

**1. How do you define success in your current role/life?**

................................................................................................

................................................................................................

................................................................................................

................................................................................................

................................................................................................

................................................................................................

................................................................................................

................................................................................................

## 2. How do you define competence?

### 3. How are these definitions making you behave?

**4. What is the cost of these behaviors, mentally, physically, emotionally, financially?**

**5. Do you believe you're serving yourself through these behaviors, or sabotaging yourself?**

Reflection is an important step toward taking action, so consider your answers carefully. The more you understand about your beliefs and behaviors, the better equipped you'll be to make positive changes in your life.

# CHAPTER FOUR

"Your workplace is rarely the source of your Imposter Syndrome, but often the trigger."

—Alison Shamir

# IMPOSTER TRIGGERS

## YOUR UNIQUE IMPOSTER EXPERIENCE

You've learned so far that ... Imposter Syndrome is a global phenomenon experienced by 70 percent of individuals. It doesn't discriminate; it isn't one-dimensional, and neither are you.

But despite its prevalence, how and why it shows up in individuals can be very different. Our life experiences vary, and each of our journeys are unique, even if they share some similarities. Imposter Syndrome is influenced by several factors, including:

- How you grew up.
- Where you grew up.
- Parents' or caregivers' actions.
- Environmental, societal, and social conditions.
- Current and previous personal relationships.

For some, Imposter Syndrome only rears its head in their personal lives, making them feel unworthy or undeserving of love and a relationship, or that they must act a certain way in order to fit in or be valued.

In the context of Imposter Syndrome, a "trigger" is akin to a button that, when pressed, activates those deep-seated feelings of fraudulence and unworthiness. These triggers vary widely and can be events, situations, scenarios, or interactions. In this chapter, we'll explore the most common triggers I've observed in my career. It's important to note that we don't often see the triggers coming, but we're always left to deal with them. Identifying and understanding your triggers is key to being able to move through the effects faster.

As mentioned, a trigger is an *event*, *situation*, *scenario*, or *interaction* you experience that then sets off your Imposter emotions and feelings.

## COMMON IMPOSTER SYNDROME TRIGGERS

Let's now discuss several common Imposter Syndrome triggers. While some may not resonate, others will be all too familiar. Often, it's a combination of factors that influence our thoughts and behavior.

Common Imposter Syndrome triggers are:

### Stepping out of your comfort zone

Whether it be a promotion, public speaking, leading a project, starting a new role or business, or venturing into uncharted territory, any action that takes you out of your comfort zone can trigger Imposter feelings. These are scenarios where you're challenging your own norms, and the resultant anxiety can reignite those deep-seated Imposter beliefs. Although stepping out of your comfort zone is a good thing, the good stops when Imposter Syndrome becomes the driver.

### Rapid success or young achievement

Consider the stories of Harry Potter Stars Daniel Radcliffe and Emma Watson—young actors thrust into huge fame and success at such early ages, which impacted their identities, leading them to later experience Imposter Syndrome.[1] The fact that anyone can adjust to that level of success is miraculous, even more so when youth is a factor. We see this play out in business scenarios too, where your achievement can mean you're the youngest in the room. Although your success is deserved, it can be a trigger. Achieving success rapidly, especially when it feels disproportionate to one's age or experience, can intensify feelings of being an Imposter. When Sylvester Stallone, a name synonymous with resilience and triumph, achieved what seemed like overnight success in 1976 with the release of *Rocky*, he suddenly leapt from the shadows of obscurity to the glaring spotlight of success. Not just any success, but the glaring spotlight of Hollywood success. While he was significantly older than the young Harry Potter stars when they found their fame, it didn't stop Imposter Syndrome from showing up. When you go from having nothing to having everything, you can feel like an Imposter. Stallone's journey is depicted in the Netflix documentary *Sly*.[2] It's a classic tale of rags to riches. To so many, his success appeared "overnight." But was it really? Or was it the culmination of relentless effort, determination, and belief in his own storytelling?

I don't want to spoil it for you because it's worth watching. Growing up with a dad and two brothers, I was exposed to many of Stallone's films. In hindsight, some were too violent for a child to be watching, but *Rocky IV* is still one of my favorite movies of all time.

Imposter Syndrome can sneak in when success seems to outpace our internal narratives of worthiness. Stallone's tough childhood, marked by neglect and abuse coming primarily from his father, ingrained a sense of inadequacy. He also received a lot of rejection and negative feedback on his worth and physical appearance throughout his childhood and young adult life. Despite this, he scripted his own destiny, carving out success with his bare hands, yet at times still questioned his worth, even when the world applauded him.

Then came the pressure to repeat success—a common occurrence with Imposter Syndrome. However, with the immense weight of global fame, that pressure was magnified. It's one thing to reach the peak; it's another to stay there. Stallone's fear mirrored what many of us feel when huge success knocks unexpectedly, even if deep down we desired it.

**The question arises, *Do I really belong here?***

This story isn't just about Stallone. It's about each of us. Success, especially when it disrupts a long-standing narrative of struggle, can feel undeserved. We attribute it to luck, timing, or other external factors, but rarely to our own merit.

The key is to internalize your achievements as much as you do your failures. This doesn't mean that Imposter Syndrome will never show up, but if it does, you'll question it, not simply believe it. So, if you've ever had fast or huge success, remember, it's not an anomaly. It's a testament to your resilience, your talent, and your hard work.

### Being in the minority

Whether it's being a woman in a male-dominated industry or representing a minority group, ethnicity, religion, culture, disability, neurodiversity, or being "the only" or "one of the few," it can magnify feelings of otherness and contribute to Imposter Syndrome.

### Firsts and onlys

Pioneering a path in your family, community, or field can be a lonely journey. Without role models or peers to relate to, "firsts" and "onlys" can feel isolated in their experiences and often feel more pressure to "represent." For example, if you're the first member of your family to go to college or move abroad, it can exacerbate feelings of being an Imposter, especially if the environment you're stepping into isn't welcoming.

### Bullying or harassment

Experiencing unfair criticism, whether in a professional or personal context, can rekindle past feelings of inadequacy and unworthiness, fueling Imposter Syndrome. I can personally attest to this one. When I was in my early twenties, I was publicly berated and humiliated by a male leader in a weekly team meeting (this man was in his late forties and the co-owner of the business). It was so bad and I was so distraught that I had to immediately exit the office. I also had to have time off work and was eventually unfairly pushed out of the business. This had a deep impact and was a huge Imposter trigger in my early career.

### External validation and its absence

Achieving accolades and recognition can paradoxically trigger Imposter Syndrome, as can the lack of recognition. The dissonance between internal feelings of inadequacy and external validation can deepen the Imposter experience.

### Competitive or toxic environments

Cultures that emphasize constant competition, a lack of healthy work-life balance, or maintain gender biases can amplify feelings of fraudulence. In trying to meet unrealistic standards, expectations, or outdated views on gender roles and perceptions of success, your sense of self can become eroded, giving rise to Imposter Syndrome. It's in these environments that your career can morph to become your identity, which is a slippery slope right into prolonged Imposter Syndrome.

### Post parental or carers' leave

For many women, returning to work after maternity leave can trigger Imposter feelings. Questions like, *Do I still belong here?* or, *Am I really adding value if I leave the office at 5 p.m.?* are common, reflecting deeper anxieties about self-worth and competence. Men are also not exempt from this and can face harsh criticism or treatment from peers should they take parental or carer's leave in cultures that aren't supportive.

### Giving or receiving constructive feedback

Embracing feedback and constructive criticism is an integral part of growth and success. Yet, for many battling Imposter Syndrome, it's a huge trigger. Imposter Syndrome ensures we internalize all feedback immediately, casting blame upon ourselves and spiraling into self-sabotaging behaviors, such as overthinking, rumination, and self-deprecation. Instead of seeing feedback as an avenue for growth, a gift, we see it as proof of our perceived inadequacies. We feel like a target. As a consequence, many shy away from seeking vital feedback and use avoidance and self-sabotaging tactics like procrastination and perfectionism to cope and protect themselves.

### Life transitions

Major life changes, such as graduating, relocating, or changing careers, can unsettle our sense of self and trigger feelings of being an Imposter. These transitions often involve new roles, expectations, and people, some of whom may, on paper, be more skilled, experienced, or intelligent (for example, they may have gotten higher grades at university). We may all of a sudden feel like a "small fish in a big pond" and start to question ourselves in new and confronting ways, rather than embracing the new environment.

### Social media influence

The curated perfection often showcased on social media platforms can create an unrealistic benchmark for personal and professional success. The constant comparison with these idealized portrayals can trigger and intensify Imposter Syndrome.

## Language and outdated phrases

Language plays a vital role in combating Imposter Syndrome—and it's not just about how we speak to ourselves. The language directed at us or that we're exposed to can be incredibly triggering. Across the business world, there are sayings that simply roll off the tongue. They're common and often designed or intended to be motivating and uplifting, but their results can in fact be the opposite.

In my previous life, I was a technology leader. I spent fifteen-plus years in commercial and sales roles for US- and Australian-founded tech companies. For ten of those years, I experienced Imposter Syndrome. Early in my career, I learned the importance (and power) of words in exacerbating fear-based emotions and behaviors. This also rings true when it comes to Imposter Syndrome.

---

*"Common phrases 'chucked around,' often out of habit, and outdated 'norms' carry implications that can feed feelings of inadequacy and Imposter Syndrome."*
*—Alison Shamir*

---

Do any of these sound familiar?

1. **"You're only as good as your last sale."** If I had a dollar for every time I heard this in my tech career, I'd be a gazillionaire. It wasn't helpful then, and it never will be. This saying implies that one's worth is only as significant as their most recent success, ignoring the cumulative effort and growth over time. It creates a high-pressure environment where past achievements are quickly forgotten and constant performance is demanded, exacerbating stress and feelings of being a fraud.

2. **"Fake it till you make it."** If you've been following my work for a while, you'll know I loathe this statement. While intended to encourage confidence, this phrase has the opposite effect. It causes you to label the action you've just taken as "fake" instead of owning and internalizing the confident steps you just took. This phrase fuels Imposter Syndrome and can be a huge confidence killer. Even with no malice intended, words have impact. More on this to come.

3. **"Leaders are born, not made."** This statement can be particularly damaging, as it suggests that leadership

qualities are innate and can't be developed. For someone striving to improve their leadership skills, this can be demoralizing, feeding into the belief that they're inherently unfit or don't belong in leadership roles.

4. **"Good things come to those who wait."** While patience is a virtue, this saying can imply that passive waiting, rather than active effort, leads to success. It can discourage proactive steps toward personal and professional growth that are essential in overcoming feelings of Imposter Syndrome, therefore leaving us questioning ourselves.

5. **"Opportunity doesn't knock twice."** This phrase can create a sense of urgency and pressure to seize every opportunity, regardless of readiness or fit. The fear of missing out can lead individuals to overextend themselves, always say "yes," or feel inadequate when they pass on opportunities.

6. **"Get out there and rattle some cages" (or the "win at all costs" viewpoint).** This can justify a ruthless, ends-justify-the-means approach in a competitive environment. It might encourage a disregard for the emotional and professional wellbeing of yourself and

> others, fostering a toxic work culture that exacerbates stress and feelings of fraudulence.

If you hear these phrases and they trigger your Imposter Syndrome, *it is valid.* These phrases can (and often do) reinforce a culture where relentless competition, constant comparison, and the masking of vulnerabilities are normalized. *They contribute to the perpetuation of Imposter Syndrome* by invalidating individual growth processes and values, encouraging unhealthy work cultures and undermining self-worth.

By identifying our Imposter triggers, we can begin to dismantle our Imposter Syndrome, manage it more effectively, and eventually overcome it. Ultimately, however, while external stimuli can fuel our Imposter experience, the true source lies within, the narratives we tell ourselves.

# CHAPTER FIVE

"Until you make the
unconscious conscious,
it will direct your life and
you will call it fate."

—Carl Jung

# IMPOSTER THINKING

## IMPOSTER THOUGHTS AREN'T FACTS

By making the unconscious conscious, we take one of the first vital steps in reclaiming our minds and brains from the grasp of Imposter Syndrome. Before we can do that, we must first understand the three levels of thinking: conscious, subconscious, and unconscious.

> **Conscious.** The conscious mind is responsible for all the thoughts and decisions you're consciously aware of. For example, when you go to a restaurant, you read the menu and consciously decide what to order, knowing why you've chosen a particular item, as the decision is calculated and deliberate. Your choice is the result of a conscious process that you can then reflect on and rationalize. Essentially, conscious thinking allows us to direct our own thoughts and actions to achieve a desired outcome.
>
> **Subconscious.** The subconscious mind holds information that can be raised up into the conscious mind when needed. It's essentially a mental storage unit filled with memories and learned processes. For example, when you need to recall the lyrics to a song or the steps to a dance, you're digging into your subconscious and bringing

that information to the surface. Importantly, you understand why that information is there in the first place.

**Unconscious.** The unconscious mind exists at a deeper level. Rather than holding memories that can be recalled and brought into the conscious mind on cue, it contains all of the unconscious thoughts, feelings, and programming you've accumulated since birth. This programming, some of which may be the result of trauma, can influence your habits and behavior and, of course, fuel Imposter Syndrome. It's the lack of awareness regarding what's happening in the unconscious mind that makes it such a tough beast to tame.[1]

Making the unconscious conscious is about intercepting the automatic fear-driven narratives and replacing them with stories rooted in reality, evidence, and self-compassion. The power of Imposter Syndrome lies in its ability to turn the brain's natural functions against us. When triggered, it sends our bodies and minds into a highly fear-based cycle. This emotional response triggers negative thoughts, which in turn fuel the emotional response, creating a relentless loop or cycle.

Imposter thinking is typically described as ANTs: automatic negative thoughts. ANTs are like uninvited guests that take up residence in our minds, whispering doubts and fears, rather than looking to the evidence of what we've achieved. This occurs because we've let the Imposter thoughts run wild for too long, allowing them to feed off the negative stories and currently embedded limiting beliefs. These thoughts are often deeply ingrained habitual thought patterns (and brain wiring) that reinforce our Imposter Syndrome.

Common examples of Imposter ANTs are:

- *Who am I to lead this team?*
- *I have no value to add.*
- *I'm lucky to be here.*
- *I can't make a mistake; they'll all know I'm a fraud.*
- *People like me don't belong in this room.*

Notice how personal this language is? These thoughts masquerade as truths, and we often accept them without question. They shape our reality, making us believe that we're less competent, less deserving, or just plain "less" than we actually are.

Ariana Huffington aptly describes this phenomenon as having an "obnoxious roommate in your head."[2] This inner critic is relentless and critical, a voice that never misses an opportunity to remind us of our perceived inadequacies.

An Imposter Syndrome voice is even more self-deprecating because we're attacking ourselves at an identity level. We're asking ourselves, *Who am I to be here?*

## THE BRAIN'S NEGATIVITY BIAS

---

*"The mind is like Velcro for negative experiences,*
*and Teflon for positive ones."*
*—Dr. Rick Hanson, Psychologist*

---

Our brains are wired with a negativity bias, a tendency to pay more attention to negative experiences over positive ones. This bias can amplify Imposter Syndrome, making negative thoughts seem more urgent and real than they actually are.

From an evolutionary standpoint, negativity bias makes sense. We have more to gain from being aware of negative stimuli than positive, the biggest gain being survival. If something is negative and potentially damaging or life-threatening, we need to know and adapt to avoid it as quickly as possible.

When making decisions, it has been shown that we naturally give more weight to the cons than the pros. Neuroscience has confirmed that the brain commits more resources to processing negative stimuli than positive stimuli.[3]

Negativity bias is an important mechanism of learning and survival, but that doesn't mean it always works in our favor. When left unchecked, it can lead to negative thoughts and feelings ruling our lives, because biologically we're wired to give them more weight.

## THE BRAIN AS A PREDICTION MACHINE

The brain also functions as a prediction machine, constantly forecasting future outcomes based on past experiences. Neuroscientist Dr. Lisa Feldman Barrett championed this once-controversial concept, describing the brain as "predictive, not reactive."[4] When it comes to Imposter Syndrome, this means that, despite evidence of success and competence, our brains are likely to predict failure or negative outcomes, because we haven't internalized our past successes, instead leading with self-sabotaging behaviors. We must disrupt these cycles.

The good news is we can rewire our brains through the power of neuroplasticity. Neuroplasticity is the automatic process of rewiring the brain through stimuli and experiences. As the term suggests, the brain is plastic, meaning it doesn't exist in a static state. It can be shaped over time, for better or worse. When you first try to learn a new skill, for example, learning to play guitar, the correct wiring isn't yet in place. You'll likely fumble your way through several lessons—or several weeks of lessons—as your brain adapts to the new experience. Gradually, new circuits form, and the once-difficult task becomes much easier, requiring less focus and effort. The more you practice a skill, the stronger and more efficient those circuits become.[5]

Our brains are constantly carrying out unconscious processes, which is both natural and necessary. The key is to understand these processes and bring them into the conscious mind. When we make the unconscious conscious, we're well on the path to reclaiming our minds from the grasp of Imposter Syndrome. It's about intercepting the automatic fear-driven narratives and replacing them with stories and behaviors rooted in reality and self-compassion.

## EMOTIONS VS. FEELINGS—WHAT'S THE DIFFERENCE?

In the intricate dance of the human psyche, emotions and feelings often seem intertwined, yet they play distinctly different roles, especially in the context of Imposter Syndrome.

Emotions are raw physical states typically triggered by external stimuli. They're the body's immediate, instinctual responses to situations. For instance, when faced with a high-stakes presentation, the initial surge of adrenaline, the quickening heartbeat, the flush of heat are all emotional responses—specifically fear responses.[6]

When discussing fear and the brain, the word "amygdala" arises. The amygdala is often called the brain's "fear center" or "emotion center." This is one simplification that has faced criticism from neuroscientists and psychologists for several reasons, and I've personally seen many individuals, facilitators, speakers, and others share outdated information and science on the topic.

The amygdala is a complex structure with various subregions, each involved in different aspects of emotional processing, including the processing of positive emotions, social interactions, and motivation. While the amygdala is involved in the fear response and other emotional reactions, it's just one piece of the overall puzzle. There are so many other factors at play, and they're not always physiological, as we covered in the Bottom-Up, Outside-In, Top-Down framework. For example, cultural and individual factors can also influence how emotions are experienced and expressed.[7]

At the heart of Imposter Syndrome lie three deeply rooted emotional reactions: shame, guilt, and embarrassment. These emotions are particularly potent because they strike at the very core of our identity and self-worth.

Shame stems from a belief that there's something fundamentally wrong with us, that we are unworthy or flawed at our core. This feeling of unworthiness often emerges when we perceive that we've failed to meet the expectations of others or, more critically, our own harsh standards.

Guilt, on the other hand, arises from the belief that we've done something wrong or that we've deceived others into believing we're more competent than we truly are. This can lead to an overwhelming sense of responsibility to maintain a facade of perfection, further fueling the cycle of fear and self-doubt.

Finally, embarrassment is the fear of being exposed, the acute discomfort of imagining others discovering the perceived gap between our public persona and our internal reality.

These emotional responses not only intensify the experience of Imposter Syndrome but also perpetuate it, creating a feedback loop that undermines our confidence and hampers our ability to authentically engage with the world. The impact of these emotions can be profound, leading to chronic stress, anxiety, and a reluctance to pursue new opportunities or take risks, ultimately limiting both personal and professional growth. Understanding and addressing these emotions is crucial for breaking free from the grip of Imposter Syndrome and reclaiming our true sense of worth.

Feelings are a step beyond emotions. They're our conscious experiences and interpretations of our emotions. Continuing with our example, the nervousness or anxiety you consciously acknowledge before a presentation is a feeling—it's your personal interpretation of the initial emotional response.[8]

As researchers Antonio Damasio and Gil B. Carvalho say, "Feelings are mental experiences of body states. They signify physiological need (for example, hunger), tissue injury (for example, pain), optimal function (for example, well-being), threats to the organism (for example, fear or anger) or specific social interactions (for example, compassion, gratitude or love)."[9]

In the realm of Imposter Syndrome, distinguishing between emotions and feelings can be a game changer. The phenomenon often triggers a visceral emotional response, a fight, flight, freeze, or fawn reaction rooted in deep-seated fears of exposure or failure. Each reaction is a response to a perceived threat. When we fight, we face the threat head-on, which could mean physically fighting or arguing aggressively. When we flee (flight), we instead attempt to avoid the threat completely, which could mean physically removing ourselves from the situation. When we freeze, as the word implies, we lock up completely to allow the threat to pass (hopefully) without any further action required. Finally, when we fawn, we submit to the threat (or person), surrendering and acquiescing to avoid conflict.[10]

While emotions do play a critical role in Imposter Syndrome, it's the internal narrative about these emotions that truly fuels Imposter thoughts. It's the difference between the instinctual stomach churn when stepping onto a stage (emotion) and the internal dialogue that follows, for example, *I don't belong here, I am scared* (feeling).

Once you understand your emotional responses to situations and the narratives that follow, you're ready to step into the control position.

## MANAGING EMOTIONS AND FEELINGS IN IMPOSTER SYNDROME

The first step toward management and taking control is to identify whether what you're experiencing is an emotion or a feeling. Is it a physical response? Or is it the story you're telling yourself about that initial response?

The language we use to label (feeling) the emotional response in our bodies has a profound impact on the next action we take. Expanding our vocabulary to express our emotions can help us push back on Imposter Syndrome while simultaneously building on our communication skills.

**Your body doesn't know the difference between FEAR and EXCITEMENT. The emotional reaction is the same; the difference is what you label it.**

## The Feeling Wheel

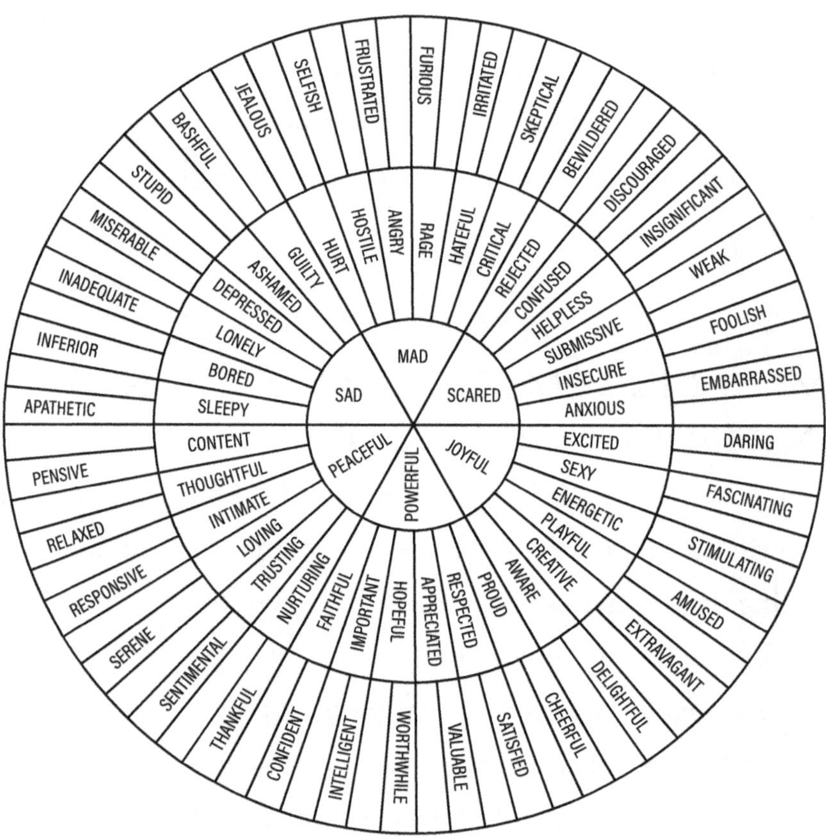


*Source: Gloria Willcox.*[11]

By using the feeling wheel, you can accurately identify the emotions you're feeling and, importantly, gain mastery over them. Whenever an emotional response is triggered, refer to the wheel to gain clarity on exactly what you're feeling. With understanding comes the ability to take control of the narrative and your Imposter Syndrome with it.

## RESPOND, DON'T REACT

---

*"Between the stimulus and response there is a space.
In that space is our power to choose our response.
In our response lies our growth and our freedom."*
*—Unknown*
*(often misattributed to Viktor Frankl and quite possibly based on his ideas)*

---

When Imposter Syndrome is in the driver's seat, we're far more reactive than responsive. Even if we hide or mask it well, we're often imploding on the inside. Allow yourself to experience the emotion without immediately weaving a narrative around it. This pause or interception can prevent the emotion from evolving into a debilitating feeling.

**Reactivity is often:**

- Immediate.
- Emotionally charged.
- Perspective-clouding, leading to self-sabotage through words or actions.
- Responsible for triggering nonverbal cues, such as facial expressions or body tension.

**When we are responsive, we:**

- Take time to process.
- Channel emotions into positive action (not self-sabotage).
- Have a rational perspective.
- Present as calm and controlled.

The goal is to learn and embrace emotional agility, and once we become aware of our triggers and tune into our bodies, we can practice navigating between emotions and feelings.

**Understand that while emotions are automatic, feelings can be managed and altered with conscious effort.**

In essence, while emotions are instinctual and often beyond our control, feelings are where we have the power to change the script. In dealing with Imposter Syndrome, mastering the dance between what we instinctively feel and what we consciously state and believe about those feelings can be the key to overcoming our fear-based responses.

## THE SCIENCE OF SELF-TALK

---

*"Your brain is like a super-computer,*
*and your self-talk is the program it will run."*
*—Jim Kwik*

---

As a mentor of mine once shared, "Words are weapons." And as I like to add, "They either serve us or sabotage us." I learned very early on in my career the power of effective communication, and how changing one word in a sentence or to yourself can make a profound impact (good or bad).

As we transition from exploring Imposter thinking, it's essential to delve deeper into the science of self-talk, going deeper than just positive affirmations. I'm talking about the intricate conversations we have with ourselves that hold profound power over our thoughts, emotions, and actions. In the world of Imposter Syndrome, self-talk isn't merely background noise; it's the engine driving the fear-based cycle or, as Jim Kwik says, the program the brain will run.

## THE NEUROSCIENCE OF SELF-TALK

Self-talk, scientifically speaking, is more than just a mental habit; it's a dynamic cognitive process deeply rooted in the brain's architecture. Research in cognitive neuroscience has shown that the prefrontal cortex, the area of the brain responsible for higher-order thinking, is heavily engaged when we engage in positive self-talk.[12] This part of the brain is tasked with processing thoughts, regulating emotions, and guiding decision-making. Positive self-talk activates the brain's reward centers, particularly the dopamine pathways. Dopamine is often referred to as the "feel-good" neurotransmitter because it's associated with feelings of pleasure, motivation, and reward. When these pathways are activated, we not only feel better but also think more clearly, make more rational decisions, and perform better under pressure.

Conversely, negative self-talk or self-criticism triggers the brain's threat detection systems, specifically the amygdala, which sends the body into a state of heightened alert, preparing us for fight or flight.[13] While our inbuilt fear-based response was evolutionarily advantageous in situations of physical danger, in the modern world, it often results in chronic stress, anxiety, and a decreased ability to perform effectively, particularly in situations that trigger Imposter Syndrome.

## THE IMPACT OF SELF-TALK ON IMPOSTER SYNDROME

Imposter Syndrome is driven by the incredibly personal and self-deprecating stories we tell ourselves and the ongoing negative self-talk that follows. Phrases like "I'm not good enough," (despite evidence that you are), "I don't deserve this," or "They're going to find out I'm a fraud" aren't just thoughts. As you've learned, they're powerful beliefs that shape how we perceive ourselves and the world around us. The negative self-talk supercharges these stories and has us still viewing the world through our Imposter mask or goggles.

This self-deprecating dialogue isn't without consequence. Repetitive negative self-talk can contribute to a range of psychological issues, including anxiety, depression, feelings of worthlessness, and impaired cognitive function. The constant reinforcement of these negative beliefs creates a feedback loop that perpetuates feelings of inadequacy and Imposterism, even in the face of evidence to the contrary.

Moreover, research in the past two years has increasingly shown that negative self-talk doesn't just affect mental health; it also has tangible effects on physical health. Chronic stress, driven by constant negative internal dialogue, has been linked to an increased risk of cardiovascular disease, weakened immune response, and clinical burnout.[14] The body and mind are inextricably connected, and the thoughts and stories we entertain and language we use toward ourselves can either support our overall wellbeing or contribute to its decline.

## THE ROLE OF SELF-TALK IN HIGH PERFORMANCE

For high achievers, the quality of self-talk can be the difference between reaching their full potential or succumbing to the pressures of their own expectations. Positive self-talk is a hallmark of resilient, high-performing individuals. It fosters a growth mindset, which is characterized by the belief that abilities and intelligence can be developed through dedication and hard work. Psychologist Carol Dweck discusses how a Chicago high school, instead of giving students a "fail" when they didn't score a passing grade, gave them a grade of "not yet." The phrase "not yet" implies that future success is possible—this isn't the end of the road!—promoting a growth mindset and a commitment to continued learning and development.[15] When you adopt a growth mindset, challenges aren't daunting, and setbacks aren't devastating.

Not only do you know you have the ability to improve, but you likely will improve.

Research shows that growth-minded individuals recover from mistakes and setbacks better than their fixed-minded counterparts. Essentially, they're more likely to achieve success. The problem with fixed-minded individuals is that they view failure as proof of their incompetence or inferiority. They don't see growth as a possibility, which can result in the avoidance of certain tasks and the abandonment of goals.[16]

Now, this is where it gets tricky, as most high-performing high achievers who experience Imposter Syndrome actually have a growth mindset. However, they face key periods of blocking themselves when triggered. The Imposter trigger has them immediately questioning themselves because it unearths long-held stories, and the self-talk turns negative almost immediately. Once we unpack our origin stories and redirect limiting beliefs, we can stay firmly in the growth mindset experience. I also have another "mindset" to share with you later ...

Many studies have highlighted that athletes who practice positive self-talk techniques significantly improve their performance outcomes compared to those who engage in neutral or negative self-talk.[17] We saw this on full display at the 2024 Paris Olympics, with many athletes caught on camera speaking to themselves and owning their moment—the moment they had worked so hard for and had earned the right to experience.

This effect isn't limited to athletes; it applies equally to professionals in high-stakes environments. When we tell ourselves, "I belong here" or, "I have value to add," we're not just offering ourselves a pep talk; we're literally rewiring our brains to approach challenges with confidence and clarity while cementing new beliefs about ourselves.

A key step in overcoming Imposter Syndrome is to become acutely aware of the self-talk patterns (stories) that dominate your internal dialogue. It requires a shift from unconscious acceptance of these thoughts to what I call conscious interception. This involves challenging the validity of the negative statements you make about yourself. In these moments of negative self-talk, it's crucial to speak back to yourself, literally. I encourage my clients to have a conversation with themselves, to literally run an intercept and question the narrative. When you add this intercept, which only requires a few seconds to action, it works as a circuit breaker, redirecting away from automatic self-sabotaging behaviors to more confident and productive action.

Redirecting self-talk involves more than just replacing negative thoughts with positive ones; it's about cultivating a narrative that's grounded in reality and evidence. This means acknowledging your successes, recognizing your efforts, and accepting your imperfections as part of the human experience. By linking your self-talk to the evidence of what you've achieved, you start to dismantle the false narratives that Imposter Syndrome thrives on.

The benefits of positive self-talk extend far beyond improved mood, motivation, and conquering Imposter Syndrome. A consistent practice of positive self-talk has been shown to enhance problem-solving abilities, increase creativity, and improve decision-making. It also promotes a healthier stress response, reducing the likelihood of burnout and improving overall wellbeing.[18] Moreover, positive self-talk has a direct impact on how we view ourselves and our place in the world. It helps reinforce a self-concept that's based on healthy views of competence, resilience, and worthiness. When we engage in positive self-talk, we're not just boosting our confidence; we're reaffirming our value and reinforcing the belief that we're capable and deserving of success.

---

*"In the battle to conquer Imposter Syndrome, self-talk is both the battlefield and the weapon to help us win."*
*—Alison Shamir*

---

By taking control of the narratives that play out in our minds, we take control of our lives. This requires a commitment to self-awareness, a willingness to challenge and change long-held beliefs, and a dedication to cultivating a narrative that empowers rather than diminishes. Remember, the story you tell yourself is the story you live. By harnessing the science of self-talk, you can rewrite your story from one of doubt and fear to one of confidence, resilience, and success. This isn't just about achieving your goals or defined success metrics; it's about owning them, celebrating them, and understanding that you're deserving of every success you achieve.

## HARNESS THE POWER OF VISUALIZATION

Anyone who knows me will tell you I'm obsessed with visualization. It's a game changer, and science now proves it.

Can you visualize your way out of Imposter Syndrome? The short answer is no. However, building on the science of self-talk, visualization and mental rehearsal are weapons that can help, and they're completely within your control. These techniques aren't just about wishful thinking or daydreaming; they're grounded in solid neuroscience and have been shown to significantly impact performance, confidence, and overall wellbeing.[19]

Visualization, at its core, is the process of creating vivid mental images of a desired outcome or scenario.

**You can win in your mind first.**

When we engage in visualization, the brain treats these mental images as if they're real experiences. This is because the same neural pathways that are activated when we physically perform an action are also engaged when we vividly imagine that action. Neuroscientists refer to this as "functional equivalence," the brain's ability to treat imagined events as though they're happening in real time.[20] For example, when an athlete visualizes themselves executing a race, it activates the same areas of the brain involved in the physical act of running, even though they aren't actually moving. This process strengthens the neural connections associated with the skill, making it easier to perform in reality. Visualization not only helps us improve certain skills, but it also accelerates the learning process. Essentially, it's a shortcut to skill mastery.

Many coaches use visualization with their clients to help guide them toward their goals. When you visualize the life you want, in your mind it's as if you've already achieved it, which subconsciously pushes you to take the relevant actions to get there for real.[21]

Research over the past few years has further validated the effectiveness of visualization. One study demonstrated that participants who regularly practiced visualization improved their physical performance almost as much as those who engaged in actual physical practice.[22] This is because visualization enhances motor skills, sharpens focus, and reduces anxiety by familiarizing the brain with the experience before it occurs.

**I have clients who have taught themselves to drive a manual car, deliver musical performances, professional talks, or presentations through the power of visualization and mental rehearsal first. Their results are remarkable.**

Closely related to visualization is mental rehearsal, a cognitive practice where you mentally walk through the steps of a task or scenario in great detail. Mental rehearsal isn't just about picturing success; it involves mentally simulating every step of the process, including potential challenges and how you'll overcome them. As a professional speaker, I mentally rehearse every step of every speaking event, including how I'll channel my emotional reactions into positive responses.

While long-term visualization supports manifesting goals, micro-visualization focuses on immediate actions. It enables quick mental rehearsal of short-term tasks or challenges, building self-belief, momentum, and fostering confidence. While we should dream big, think big, and visualize big, we should do it all at the micro level too.

The power of mental rehearsal lies in its ability to prepare the brain for success. When you mentally rehearse a scenario, you're essentially creating a blueprint for your brain to follow when the actual event occurs. This reduces the brain's cognitive load during the real event because it has already "practiced" the scenario. This is particularly beneficial in high-pressure situations where Imposter Syndrome might otherwise trigger solely fear-based visions. You should start by preparing and rehearsing for a positive outcome, not the worst-case scenario, which is where your Imposter Syndrome may try to push you. The key is to push back, leading with the positive or best possible outcome. This is the same when someone asks, "Do you want the good news or the bad news?" Always start with the good.

Studies have shown that mental rehearsal can also help in managing and reducing anxiety.[23] By mentally rehearsing a successful outcome, you condition your brain to expect positive results, which in turn can decrease the likelihood of panic or self-sabotage when you're faced with the actual task. This technique is especially powerful for those struggling with Imposter Syndrome, as it can help rewire the brain's automatic response from one of fear and inadequacy to one of confidence, competence, and capability.

For individuals dealing with Imposter Syndrome, visualization and mental rehearsal offer a way to counteract the negative self-talk and limiting beliefs that often hold them back. By consistently visualizing successful outcomes and mentally rehearsing your performance, you can begin to reprogram your internal narrative, which is essential when conquering Imposter Syndrome.

Visualization and mental rehearsal aren't just about picturing yourself at the finish line; they're about mentally experiencing every part of the journey, starting with the best outcome. Then once you've mastered this, you can move on to including the obstacles and seeing yourself navigate them successfully. This practice builds resilience, reduces the fear of failure, and reinforces the belief that you're capable and deserving of success.

Incorporating these techniques into your daily routine can significantly enhance your ability to manage Imposter Syndrome as you become adept at intercepting and redirecting fear-based emotional reactions to more positive and proactive visions and actions. Each time we take a positive mental or physical step, we're retraining and rewiring our brains for the greater good.

With the right knowledge (for example, understanding negativity bias, the difference between emotions and feelings, and the neuroscience of self-talk) and the right tools (for example, positive self-talk, visualization, and mental rehearsal), you can begin to reshape your Imposter experience into a powerful new perspective, fueled by confidence, self-worth, and an unwavering belief in your ability to succeed.

# CHAPTER SIX

"Conquering Imposter Syndrome is not a 'quick fix,' but it isn't a life sentence either. Once we understand our Imposter cycle, we can intercept and redirect it."

—Alison Shamir

# IMPOSTER BEHAVIORS

## IMPOSTER PERSONAS AND ANCHORING TO AUTHENTICITY

Imposter Syndrome doesn't just linger in the mind; it's embedded in our actions, behaviors, and routines. Once the mental cycle of negative self-talk takes root, it begins to influence how we behave in our everyday lives. Often, these behaviors become habitual, ingrained responses that seem to offer protection but instead trap us in a cycle of self-sabotage. These are the behaviors that keep Imposter Syndrome alive and well, fostering a false sense of security while blocking us from reaching our full potential and standing as our authentic selves. We adopt what I call an "Imposter persona".

These personas act like shields or masks, as Dr. Pauline Clance discusses in *The Impostor Phenomenon*, allowing us to perform but also "protecting us" from anyone finding out that we're not as smart, talented, capable, or successful *as they believe us to be.*[1] Each time we act from our persona, Imposter Syndrome pulls us away from authenticity with the fundamental driver being the story we tell ourselves. If left unchecked, that story controls our thoughts, our behaviors, and has us viewing and measuring competence in unhealthy ways. At times, it's a relentless and always negative cycle.

## FIVE IMPOSTER TYPES AND THE COMPETENCE CONNECTION

When it comes to viewing competence through the lens of Imposter Syndrome, author and fellow expert Dr. Valerie Young's research has highlighted five different competence types (commonly referred to as the five types of Imposter Syndrome) each with its own unique focus: the perfectionist, the expert, the soloist, the natural genius, and the superhuman. Here's how Valerie describes each type … *do any of these resonate with you?*

- **The perfectionist's** primary focus is on "how" something is done. This includes how the work is conducted and how it turns out. One minor flaw in an otherwise stellar performance, or 99 out of 100, equals failure and thus shame.

- **The expert** is the knowledge version of the perfectionist. Here, the primary concern is on "what" and "how much" they know or can do. Because they expect to know everything, even a minor lack of knowledge denotes failure and shame.

- **The soloist** cares mostly about "who" completes the task. To make it on the achievement list, it has to be them and them alone. Because they think they need to do and figure out everything on their own, needing help is a sign of failure that evokes shame.

- **The natural genius** also cares about "how" and "when" accomplishments happen, but for them competence is measured in terms of ease and speed. The fact that they have to struggle to master a subject or skill or that they're not able to bang out their masterpiece on the first try equals failure, which evokes shame.

- **The superhuman** measures competence based on "how many" roles they can both juggle and excel in. Falling short in any role—as a manager, team member, parent, partner, friend, volunteer—evokes shame because they feel they should be able to handle it all perfectly and easily.[2]

So, how does all this play out in practice?

My "Imposter persona" and view of competence was tied to being a perfectionist. This was a way of "protecting myself" so no one "found out" I wasn't really capable. I found myself always striving for perfection and seeking external validation to make myself look and feel better. But even when I achieved a perfect score or won an award, it was **never enough.** My Imposter Syndrome told me I had gotten lucky or I still wasn't good enough. I couldn't internalize my success, and I just kept chasing more and more. I was on a constant quest for better performance, even when I was performing at my best. It was a relentless cycle based on an unattainable goal. I was always doomed to feel like I was failing.

When it comes to performance, each gender can react differently to performance cues and conditions, such as negative feedback and accountability. For instance, while both genders feel distress when they feel they're underperforming or not meeting expectations, men can experience higher stress levels when given negative feedback and perform worse in high-accountability situations.[3] While both genders view competence through a similar Imposter lens, their reactions to what they see are very different, highlighting the complex and nuanced nature of the phenomenon.

## UNDERSTANDING IMPOSTER CYCLES

Research on Imposter Syndrome reveals that it follows a predictable cycle for individuals. This cycle typically begins with a trigger, as covered in chapter four. When the trigger occurs, individuals with Imposter Syndrome often experience a deep emotional reaction and spike in anxiety, self-doubt, and feelings of unworthiness. When it's time to perform, some may delay starting a task, feeling stuck and unable to move forward, while others may overcompensate by beginning early and giving themselves far too long of a runway, which in itself can be draining. Those who procrastinate often end up rushing to complete their work under pressure, fueled by panic. Overpreparers tend to believe their success is due to extreme and unsustainable preparation, while those who procrastinate put it down to luck. While associating achievement with hard work may seem positive, the problem is, individuals with Imposter Syndrome don't believe that hard work is a true measure of ability. They don't see their success as genuine or earned.

Overworking is another common Imposter behavior. Individuals with Imposter Syndrome may spend more time and energy on a task than necessary to get good results, which means other tasks get neglected. Even when, deep down, they understand that the extra effort is unnecessary, the cycle of overworking is difficult to break. They've grown accustomed to the approach and struggle to accept that they can get results without it. Why risk it?

Once the project has been completed and the outcome praised, which often occurs, an individual may feel a sense of relief before happiness. However, this relief is short-lived, and when a new challenge arises, they fall back into the same cycle, dismissing their previous successes.[4] Over time, they come to believe that enduring this cycle of stress and self-doubt is a prerequisite for success. This belief reinforces the Imposter cycle, making it incredibly hard to escape. We can't win.

## The Imposter Cycle

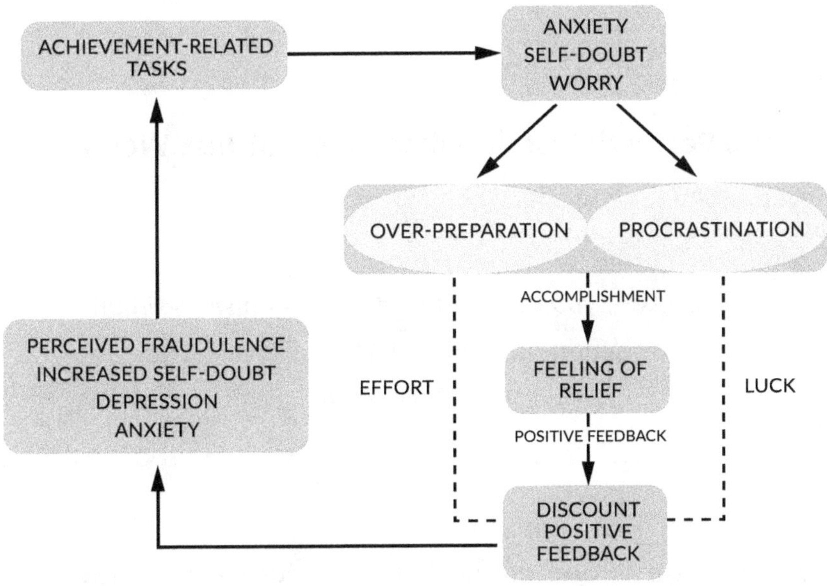


*Source: International Journal of Behavioral Science.*[5]

## COMMON SELF-SABOTAGING BEHAVIORS IN IMPOSTER SYNDROME

When it comes to Imposter Syndrome, there are several self-sabotaging behaviors individuals tend to adopt: comparison, people-pleasing, overworking, rumination, avoidance, procrastination, and the big one—perfectionism. Some of us could tick every one off the list. Daunting, I know. While these behaviors are common and can be difficult to alter, the good news is, they *can* be changed. You *can* break the cycle. To change something, we must first understand it. Let's start with perfectionism.

### The Perfectionist Paradigm (It's Not Just Women)

---

*"Imposter-Syndrome-induced perfectionism is simply fear masquerading as excellence."*
*–Alison Shamir*

---

Perfectionism is one of the hallmark behaviors of Imposter Syndrome, driven by an intense need to prove worth through flawless performance. Individuals caught in this trap believe that any mistake is a sign of incompetence. As a result, they set unrealistic standards for themselves, overworking and obsessing over details to prevent any perceived "flaw." Ironically, perfectionism often leads to diminished productivity while fueling burnout and a perpetual dissatisfaction with one's work. The cycle is self-perpetuating: the harder they push for perfection, the more they reinforce the idea that anything less would expose their "true" inadequacies. If left unchecked, perfectionism can lead to depression, addiction, and other personality disorders.[6] It can have a dark side.

Before we go any further, let me bust another myth: perfectionism isn't just experienced by women (neither is Imposter Syndrome, as you've learned by now). You can also experience perfectionism without it being Imposter Syndrome.

A common question is also: *can perfectionism be a positive trait?* Yes, it can, when it's an internal motivation to do your best. Take school for example. In our formative school years, the level we need to achieve for a "perfect" result is usually clear-cut, for example, getting an A-plus. But as we move into adult life, the measure of perfection isn't always so clear:

- What is the perfect sale or project result?
- What do you call a perfect success?
- What is a perfect speech?

You see, in the adult world, defining "perfect" is much harder, and, at a certain point, perfectionism can move from healthy to unhealthy. If it's fueled by Imposter Syndrome, it's absolutely sabotaging you.

### Perfectionism Comes in Three Flavors

Let's look at some of the psychology and science behind perfectionism. So, what are the three main types of perfectionism? In the 1990s, psychologists Dr. Paul Hewitt and Dr. Gordon Flett defined three main types of perfectionism:

- Self-oriented perfectionism (high expectations of yourself).
- Other-oriented perfectionism (high expectations of others).
- Socially prescribed perfectionism (belief that others have high expectations of you).[7]

**Self-oriented perfectionism** presents as setting extremely high (and often unrealistic) expectations on oneself. For some people, this can be motivating to a point, as it gives them a drive to be the best. But in other people, self-oriented perfectionism can lead to self-sabotaging behaviors.

The question here becomes: is the goal achievable and measurable? If the goal is to achieve 100 percent on a math test, or a perfect 10.0 score in a gymnastics competition, there's an objective measure of success to aim for. Whether the person achieved the perfect score, or not, is measurable, and more than one person can achieve a perfect score on the same test.

But if the goal is vague or subjective, a person with self-oriented perfectionist tendencies can find themselves pursuing a goal they'll never reach. This behavior can be toxic, and, as we know, a business environment isn't a math test nor a gymnastics arena.

Self-oriented perfectionism can show up as procrastination, indecisiveness, shame, and low self-esteem. It's also associated with anxiety, depression, and eating disorders. Self-oriented perfectionists are constantly trying to close the gap between their perceived real self and their ideal self. While there's nothing wrong with self-improvement, you shouldn't place any unrealistic expectations on yourself. When expectations are too high—the hallmark of the self-oriented perfectionist—failure to meet such impossible standards can negatively affect mental health.[8]

**Other-oriented perfectionism** presents as placing high importance on other people in one's life being perfect, for example, having unrealistic expectations regarding a subordinate's performance at work or a partner's behavior in a relationship. This can show up in two ways.

At a healthy level, other-oriented perfectionism can drive people to be great leaders and team motivators. They have high expectations of their teams, and with a supportive and inspiring attitude, their teams can excel.

At an unhealthy level, it can show up as blame, lack of trust, and hostility toward others. Other-oriented perfectionists can become the types of leaders who are never satisfied, even when the team achieves the goal they were aiming for.[9] Such leaders often keep moving the goalposts, which can frustrate the people they're leading, as the team can never win.

Finally, in cases of **socially prescribed perfectionism**, individuals believe that significant people in their lives have high expectations of them and are exerting pressure on them to be perfect. They feel that no matter how hard they try, they'll never meet others' unrealistic expectations. This can be particularly hurtful when it's a family member or loved one who has impossibly high expectations.

Socially prescribed perfectionism can result in feelings of anger, anxiety, and depression. Individuals fear negative evaluation, and they avoid earning disapproval of others at all costs.[10]

## Other Factors of Perfectionism

Some people experience thoughts and behaviors that overlap all three types of perfectionism. People who are high on all forms of perfectionism have been described as neurotic perfectionists.[11]

Additionally, people with narcissistic personality traits often strive for perfection, both for themselves and for other people in their lives. They push people to achieve unrealistic levels of perfection while hiding their own imperfections from others. Essentially, they seek to appear perfect—an impossible ideal—and expect others to meet the same standard, even though it isn't genuine or achievable.[12] When perfectionism is weaponized or fueled by narcissism, perfectionists can be a tough crowd to be around.

Now that we understand *what* perfectionism is and how it commonly presents, it's time to ask the question: where do perfectionist tendencies come from?

## The Origin of Perfectionist Tendencies

In most cases, perfectionism starts in early childhood and is then impacted (or compounded) by social and environmental factors as we grow. When someone's parent, guardian, relative, or teacher is a perfectionist or, worse, a narcissist who has high (and unreasonable) expectations of the child, the person can develop perfectionist tendencies of their own. This is likely to show up as socially prescribed perfectionism. In my case, I was neglected as a child, which made me turn to perfectionism as a way of trying to get my mother's attention. That was, until the abuse I suffered grew so intense and extensive that perfectionism then became a coping mechanism tied to "control."

Every perfectionist's behavior and origin are different.

Another key factor (despite the progress we've made in modern times) is that large parts of society continue to encourage girls to be perfect, well-mannered, obedient, a "good girl" rather than the brave, boundary-pushing risk-takers they encourage young boys to be.

An extensive study by the LEGO Group found that girls as young as five already feel societal pressure to be "perfect," hindering their confidence and creativity. Much of the problem stems from the language we use. For instance, as a society, we're seven times more likely to use words like sweet, pretty, cute, and beautiful to describe girls than boys. When it comes to boys, we're twice as likely to use words like brave, cool, genius, and innovative. As girls get older, perfectionist tendencies increase, as does anxiety around failure and making mistakes. Over time, they lose confidence in their creativity and hesitate to share their ideas. To address the issue, researchers are calling for a change in the language we use to describe young girls.[13] Why can't girls be brave, cool, genius, and innovative too? They can—they often are, in fact—and it's time we let them know it. It's time we stopped conditioning young girls to place unrealistic expectations upon themselves, setting them up for perfectionism and self-sabotage later in life. Yes, this conditioning carries on into adulthood.

Further research focusing on college students found that women exhibit greater levels of self-sabotaging perfectionism than men, likely due to the higher expectations they place upon themselves.[14] It's that same conditioning at play again. Clearly, it's not something we can simply escape with age. The conditioning itself must be consciously reversed.

**Of course, men aren't exempt from perfectionism or Imposter Syndrome.** They do, however, experience it differently from women. In his book, *The Perfection Trap*, Thomas Curran discusses exactly how perfectionism affects men, though the broader societal focus often leans toward its impact on women. Curran highlights that perfectionism is a significant issue for men as well, with distinct challenges and pressures that are often less-openly discussed.[15]

Through my discussions with men, I've identified several reasons perfectionism can show up for them:

- **Societal expectations.** Men experience perfectionism due to societal expectations that demand high achievement, stoicism, and a strong outward image. The pressure to meet these expectations can lead men to internalize a need to be perfect in their professional and personal lives.

- **Performance pressure.** Perfectionism in men is often closely tied to performance, especially in careers, sports, and concerning physical appearance. The expectation to be the best, earn the most, or be the strongest can lead to chronic stress and anxiety.

- **Emotional suppression.** Traditional masculine norms discourage men from expressing vulnerability, leading to suppressed emotions. This emotional suppression can exacerbate perfectionist tendencies, as men may feel they can't afford to show weakness or imperfection.

- **Workplace dynamics.** In professional settings, men can face intense pressure to succeed and may equate their self-worth with their career achievements. This can lead to burnout, workaholism, and a constant fear of failure (not to mention prolonged Imposter Syndrome).

- **Cultural conditioning.** That's right—men aren't exempt from cultural conditioning. From a young age, they're often conditioned to associate their value with achievement, strength, and success. This

> cultural conditioning makes them more prone to perfectionist behaviors as they strive to meet these ideals.

The pressure to meet impossible standards without showing strain can lead to severe emotional and psychological consequences.

At its core, Imposter Syndrome fueled perfectionism is the relentless pursuit of flawlessness and setting excessively high standards for oneself, yet never being satisfied.

As you can see, perfectionism has close links to Imposter Syndrome. However, the core motivations behind each tendency can vary. For instance, some perfectionists (all genders) are driven by a strong internal desire to meet their high standards rather than a fear of being exposed as a fraud. These individuals may feel confident in their abilities but are constantly striving for improvement and excellence. They're never satisfied but don't necessarily feel like a fraud or fear exposure if they don't get a perfect result. You can be excessively driven by perfectionism but not necessarily have the catastrophic thinking patterns often associated with Imposter Syndrome and perfectionist tendencies combined. Perfectionists can be confident in their abilities and not question their worth or legitimacy. They can still recognize their achievements and feel a sense of pride, even if they're never fully satisfied with the results.

## Achievement vs. Inadequacy

A perfectionist without Imposter Syndrome may be more focused on the achievement itself rather than worrying about whether they deserve the recognition. They might be driven by a passion for excellence or a desire for mastery, without the underlying anxiety that characterizes Imposter Syndrome, which is where I'm at today, having conquered my own Imposter Syndrome. However, the perfectionist tendencies remain; I just know how to control them.

Recently, a very large corporate client described me *as a perfectionist* in her testimonial following my delivery of an Imposter Syndrome masterclass. I saw this as a huge compliment because it demonstrated to me that I've redirected my self-sabotaging perfectionism into striving for excellence. I was also able to internalize this testimonial and all others I receive because I've conquered my Imposter Syndrome.

While perfectionism and Imposter Syndrome can overlap, they're distinct constructs. Perfectionism, at its extreme, can be debilitating, but there are some situations where perfectionism can be healthy and help you strive to be your best. I want to help you know the difference so you can recognize the benefits and warning signs in your own behavior.

When perfectionism supports your efforts rather than derailing you, it can be a positive trait. In some situations, perfectionism can drive you to try harder and do better than previous efforts. This can be wonderful, because it might be the final push you need to go beyond what you thought was possible. However, if your pursuit of perfection leads to self-sabotaging behaviors, such as chronic procrastination, then it's no longer serving you.

If you're unsure whether your perfectionism is presenting in a healthy or unhealthy way, ask the question: *Do I feel good about myself?* When you aim for—and achieve—the perfect outcome (the goal you set), how do you feel? Do you feel good about yourself and your achievement? Or do you feel deflated and disappointed in the result? If you feel great and can celebrate your epic achievement, you're experiencing the positive side of perfectionism. However, if achieving your goal makes you feel awful or discontent, or relief without the joy, then your perfectionism is presenting in an unhealthy way. You may decide that the goal you set yourself wasn't ambitious enough. In this case, your perfectionist traits are making you miserable instead of happy, which means something needs to change.

So, how can you draw the line between healthy and unhealthy perfectionism? It starts by conquering Imposter Syndrome.

## BEYOND PERFECTIONISM—OTHER SELF-SABOTAGING BEHAVIORS

Although perfectionism is often the global poster child for self-sabotaging behavior linked to Imposter Syndrome, it isn't the only one. Let's now explore the other common behaviors that keep us trapped in the Imposter cycle. It's important to note, these are gender-agnostic.

**Comparison** is another pervasive behavior that keeps individuals feeling "less than." With Imposter Syndrome, comparison is often skewed and biased. Instead of viewing others' success as inspiration, individuals with Imposter Syndrome see it as proof of their own inferiority. They constantly measure themselves—their achievements and their skills—against others, creating a distorted perspective. This comparison magnifies feelings of inadequacy, driving self-doubt deeper and making individuals feel as though they're in a constant state of "catching up" instead of connecting with the evidence of their success.

**People-pleasing** is another common self-sabotaging behavior. Driven by a fear of disapproval or rejection, many with Imposter Syndrome resort to people-pleasing as a defense mechanism. They go out of their way to gain validation and approval, often at the expense of their own needs and boundaries. People-pleasing can lead to overcommitting, saying "yes" when "no" would be more appropriate, and neglecting self-care. In an effort to please everyone, they lose sight of their own identity and reinforce the idea that they're only valuable when others are happy with them.

**Overworking** is a form of self-sabotage that stems from the belief that constant effort will eventually make an individual "worthy" of their position. By putting in excessively long hours and taking on more than is reasonable, they hope to prove their competence. However, overworking often results in exhaustion, stress, and even resentment. Worse yet, no amount of effort seems to quiet the automatic negative thoughts (ANTs), leading to a cycle of working harder and harder without feeling any more competent. There are also certain workplaces and environments where this is exacerbated, which I discuss further in chapter seven.

**Rumination** is the mental habit of replaying a situation over and over, analyzing every perceived mistake or flaw. For those with Imposter Syndrome, rumination can become a near-constant state of mind. This behavior traps them in a loop of negative self-reflection, reinforcing their sense of inadequacy. Ruminating also keeps their focus on past "failures" rather than future growth, feeding the cycle of self-doubt and perpetuating feelings of unworthiness.

**Avoidance** is a strategy of self-protection that almost always backfires. When individuals avoid tasks, challenges, or opportunities due to fear of failure, they reinforce their

Imposter beliefs. While avoidance offers temporary relief, it ultimately confirms their sense of inadequacy by preventing them from proving their capabilities. Over time, avoidance limits growth, stifles potential, and deepens the fear of taking on new challenges.

**Procrastination**, unlike avoidance, which is a direct refusal to engage, involves delaying action on tasks or responsibilities, often under the guise of "waiting for the right time" or "needing to feel ready." For individuals with Imposter Syndrome, procrastination is frequently fueled by perfectionism and fear of failure. The underlying thought is, *If I don't start, I can't fail* or, *If I delay, I can buy more time to do it perfectly*. This behavior often leads to a vicious cycle. The task remains incomplete; anxiety builds as deadlines loom, and the individual eventually scrambles to finish under pressure. The result may be rushed or subpar work, which reinforces the belief that they're incapable or undeserving. Alternatively, even if the work is successful, the individual attributes it to luck or last-minute effort, rather than their abilities, perpetuating feelings of fraudulence.

Procrastination also drains mental energy, as the lingering weight of unfinished tasks occupies headspace and saps motivation. Over time, it can lead to decreased productivity, increased stress, and missed opportunities, all of which reinforce the Imposter cycle. Breaking free from procrastination involves recognizing it as a form of self-sabotage and addressing the underlying fears driving the delay, rather than relying on temporary avoidance as a coping mechanism.

## BREAKING THE CYCLE

No matter who we are, where we come from, or how prevalent Imposter Syndrome has been for us, we all have an origin story (and now you know how to identify yours). We all have a default ANT (Automatic Negative Thought), the way the story plays out in your head (by identifying it, you can then intercept it). We all have an Imposter cycle we must break (once you identify the story that fuels it, you can intercept it and redirect the self-sabotage to a new behavior that serves you).

It's essential to recognize these patterns of self-sabotage and understand that they're learned behaviors, not truths. The first step in breaking the cycle is to identify these behaviors as they arise. Becoming aware of how Imposter Syndrome manifests through actions like perfectionism and overworking allows us to confront them with a clearer mind.

Each of these behaviors is driven by the need to protect ourselves from feeling vulnerable, exposed, or inadequate. Yet, by engaging in these habitual patterns, we give power to Imposter Syndrome, allowing it to dictate our actions and define our worth. We stay in the "Imposter persona" and lose track of who we really are. Recognizing these behaviors is a powerful act of self-awareness. It allows us to pause and ask:

**"Is this behavior serving or sabotaging me?"**

In the final chapter, we'll delve into practical techniques to intercept these behaviors and replace them with habits that support self-worth, confidence, and authenticity. It's a process that requires patience and commitment but ultimately frees us from the constraints of Imposter Syndrome, allowing us to embrace our achievements with a genuine sense of pride.

# CHAPTER SEVEN

"When 70 percent of individuals experience Imposter Syndrome, it's not just an individual issue; it's an organizational one too."

—Alison Shamir

# IMPOSTERIZATION™
## (Workplaces, Systems, Structures, and DEI)

## IMPOSTER TRIGGERS IN THE WORKPLACE—A FAMILIAR STORY

Picture this—you're at the top of your game, working in a senior role at a global company, lots of travel, amazing office, executive salary, perks, and an awesome team to boot! Sounds like a corporate dream, right? It was, for a while, and then one day it all changed.

There was a new director in town, a sharp-talking chauvinist who loved a weeknight drink and was full of brash and ego. He was the poster boy of the company and seemingly untouchable—an all too familiar scenario.

I was the only female in the team, and I was firmly in his sights. He didn't care for women much, and he certainly didn't like it when they held leadership positions. At first, the bullying was sold as "constructive criticism," but I knew better. My instincts told me there was more to it. *But my Imposter Syndrome was firmly back in control.* Fast-forward a few months, and I was living and working in denial. The bullying had intensified. I second-guessed myself constantly, and I was again firmly in a self-sabotaging cycle led by Imposter Syndrome. It was a dark time, and it didn't end well for me. My high-flying career came crashing down in what seemed like an instant. I was anxious; I was burnt out; I felt lost. The anxiety, the self-doubt, the fear of being found out as a fraud all pushed me closer to the edge, culminating in more panic attacks as I battled my negative thoughts.

I've come to realize that this is still a familiar story to many.

No matter the gender of the bully, bullying can trigger Imposter Syndrome big time, as touched on in chapter four when we discussed Imposter triggers.

It took me two years to recover from this experience. It impacted my self-worth, self-esteem, and self-confidence so greatly that I was questioning my entire career. *What should I do next? How will I pay my mortgage? Who would want to hire me now?* My internal narrative was negative and relentless. It was so grossly unfair because I suffered, and he didn't.

You might be asking, *Did you push back on him?* I did, eventually, but the company protected him, throwing me under the bus.

It was never my fault. But that didn't make it any less triggering.

As you know, we all have an individual journey with Imposter Syndrome, one shaped by nature and nurture. But how does Imposter Syndrome play out in work environments? And what can be done to navigate it?

## THE ROLE OF DIVERSITY, EQUITY, AND INCLUSION (DEI)

Diversity, equity, and inclusion (DEI) are crucial for individuals overcoming Imposter Syndrome because inclusive environments validate diverse identities, experiences, and contributions, reducing the isolation, fears, and doubts that fuel Imposter feelings. When organizations prioritize equity, they dismantle systemic biases and barriers that disproportionately impact underrepresented groups, creating spaces where individuals feel valued for who they are, not just what they achieve. By fostering psychological safety and encouraging open dialogue, DEI initiatives empower individuals to challenge the internal narratives of inadequacy and insecurity, replacing them with a sense of belonging and confidence in their abilities. In essence, DEI provides the cultural and structural support that complements personal efforts to break free from the cycle of Imposter Syndrome.

We spend approximately one-third of our lives at work. For some of us, it feels like even more. I remember leaving my corporate role in 2019 to start my own business, and it felt like I was working 24/7 for the first three years. I'm happy to say that I've found a better balance in recent years. Because work consumes such a large portion of our lives, it can have a massive influence over us. Our environments matter, especially those where we spend most of our time. Whether we work for ourselves or within the structures of organizations and institutions, our professional environments have a significant impact on our Imposter experience.

In order to navigate Imposter Syndrome, we must understand the role of the environment and the triggers, and carve our own path through. Even if you find yourself in a toxic environment, I understand that, chances are, you can't just leave. You've worked hard to get there, years in fact, so it's not as simple as just walking away. Once we understand the environmental impacts, we can learn to navigate them. That doesn't mean they don't need to, or shouldn't, change—of course change is needed, but my goal right now is to give you a choice and place the power back in your hands.

## IMPOSTER SYNDROME FUELED BY BIAS AND DISCRIMINATION

As we know, Imposter Syndrome can affect anyone of any race or gender. We're not talking about a phenomenon that only affects women or isn't relevant to people of color. Imposter Syndrome is a *human* issue, and we can't discount anyone's experience with it, nor attach it to a single group. It's a pervasive phenomenon that can strike anyone, especially when certain environmental factors are at play.

Psychologist and researcher Kevin Cokley points out that while some people of color who may be experiencing Imposter

Syndrome struggle to identify with their diagnosis, it doesn't mean they aren't suffering from the phenomenon.[1] In his own research, he notes that early studies of Imposter Syndrome mainly focused on White women and failed to consider factors such as race and racial discrimination that could contribute to the phenomenon in other groups, especially minorities. With this in mind, Cokley and colleagues set out to expand the original model to be more culturally informed, identifying five key themes relevant to Black graduate students that underlie Imposter Syndrome: awareness of low racial representation, questioning intelligence, expectations, psychosocial costs, and explaining success externally.[2]

Essentially, when a minority group feels underrepresented—for example, in the classroom or workplace—it fuels feelings of not belonging, which can lead to Imposter Syndrome. Additionally, minorities and marginalized groups often have high expectations placed upon them by others, especially when they're considered high achievers. When performance doesn't match expectations, whether real or imagined, it can lead to feeling like an Imposter. Further, when they don't see others like them consistently succeeding—for example, graduating college or receiving big promotions—they can begin to question their own intelligence.[3] *Should I even be here?* they ask. The doubt can be crippling. While self-doubt despite evidence of competence is a prominent trait of Imposter

Syndrome across the board, minorities can, and often do, experience it for different reasons than other groups, which is important to consider when working to conquer the phenomenon.

Research also shows that minorities may experience the "psychological costs" of Imposter Syndrome, such as anxiety and overworking, for different reasons than those in non-marginalized groups. While they may work hard to avoid being outed as a fraud, they also seek to shatter negative stereotypes, often around their intelligence, ability, or belonging.[4] Just like many women have been conditioned to believe they need to be perfect, fueling Imposter feelings when they don't meet such a high standard, many people of color have been conditioned to believe they aren't worthy of success, which can fuel Imposter Syndrome when they start succeeding. They often end up attributing their success to external sources, such as faith, social support, and rechanneled oppression.[5] While all groups exhibit similar Imposter behaviors, the triggering environmental factors, such as the racism and racial bias that affect people of color, can vary.

We've previously discussed how men and women experience Imposter Syndrome differently and how gender conditioning can fuel perfectionist tendencies, but there's another piece of the puzzle. As highlighted by my tale of workplace bullying, gender discrimination can also be a factor, as can a phenomenon called gender stigma consciousness.

When an individual has acute gender stigma consciousness, they believe they'll be judged based on their gender rather than their abilities. They're conscious of the fact that their gender is stigmatized or discriminated against in certain situations and environments, which leads to poorer performance. The perpetuating stereotype that men are more competent than women in certain areas that are critical to society, such as STEM fields, has potentially led to a higher prevalence of gender stigma consciousness in women.[6] With this in mind, it's easy to see how Imposter Syndrome could arise in women who step into these fields. They're fighting an uphill battle from the start against gender bias, discrimination, and their own conditioned beliefs. No wonder they often feel like Imposters.

Interestingly, it's not just women who suffer the effects. Research shows that gender stigma consciousness is associated with Imposter Syndrome in both women *and* men. When individuals are acutely aware of their gender's stereotypes, they're more likely to dwell and even act on them, which can lead to feeling like an Imposter.[7] They believe that their gender can't excel in certain areas, and this belief becomes a self-fulfilling prophecy as, consequently, their performance suffers. This doesn't negate the serious impact of a toxic environment. However, my aim is to share insights into multiple real-world experiences.

Just as the workplace triggers for Imposter Syndrome can vary across groups, so can the remedies. For instance, while male "Imposters" see and internalize a promotion as external validation of their abilities, diminishing Imposter feelings, women often don't.[8] They can't achieve their way out of Imposter Syndrome, while men often find some relief in success and validation.

No person's or group's experience with Imposter Syndrome is the same, and it's important that we look beyond the individual to also consider the cultural and environmental factors at play. As I've said before, and will likely say again, Imposter Syndrome isn't one-dimensional. It's a complex web that takes deep understanding and conscious effort to untangle. When it comes to Imposter Syndrome, knowledge really is power. It's in understanding the nuances of the phenomenon that we find the means to conquer it.

## IMPOSTER SYNDROME'S PENCHANT FOR HIGH-PRESSURE FIELDS

While Imposter Syndrome can appear in any professional setting, its effects are particularly amplified in fields and industries marked by systemic structures, high stakes, and intense expectations, which all create fertile ground for Imposter feelings to emerge.

**To recap, some of the hallmarks of Imposter Syndrome are:**

- Perfectionist tendencies, which include setting unrealistic expectations on yourself, harsh self-criticism, and never being satisfied (even if you produce a good result).
- Excessive fear of failure, mistakes, and criticism, which leads to catastrophic thinking.
- The constant need and quest for external validation and approval or to "be the best," driven by fear not ambition.

* * *

It's easy to see how certain environments can be melting pots for the Imposter Phenomenon. These environments are more than just competitive; they often come with deeply ingrained biases, hierarchical cultures, and significant external pressures that exacerbate the triggers and symptoms of Imposter Syndrome. Such environments demand constant excellence, leave little room for vulnerability, and often fail to provide the psychological safety needed to combat feelings of inadequacy. Not to mention the often overlooked but deeply impactful sleep deprivation caused by long hours and the "always on" mentality in our 24/7 digital world.

For high-performing individuals in these environments, overcoming their relentless Imposter cycle can feel like an impossible dream, a shadow too broad and consuming to ever escape. But it doesn't have to be this way. Once we understand our journey with Imposter Syndrome, we can move from self-blame to self-awareness, compassion, and mastery. Yes, self-mastery, because although we can't always control our environments, we can control our responses to them. I'm not suggesting it's easy. In fact, I've not once said overcoming Imposter Syndrome is easy, but it's certainly possible and absolutely worth it. Despite your journey being unique (because there's only one you), you can learn a lot by studying other environments, and you can certainly feel less alone.

Let's explore some of the high-pressure fields where Imposter Syndrome is prevalent.

But before we do, it's important to note that, in these fields, it's "not all bad". Individuals working in these environments can and do have very fulfilling careers that they love, and organizations, teams, and leaders across these fields and sectors can create and lead wonderful dynamic cultures of growth. I'm not putting everyone in the same bucket, nor trying to paint a bleak picture, because Imposter Syndrome can and does exist in psychologically safe high- and low-pressure environments too. While environments and workplaces do play a role, they're not the sole cause of Imposter Syndrome, as it's driven primarily by your origin story and the ongoing negative stories you tell yourself. The environments are secondary but, as you've learned, still very important to your journey and Imposter experience. To truly conquer Imposter Syndrome, we must look at both individual and environmental factors so you feel truly empowered to understand and embrace your own journey.

### Medicine

Medicine is one of the most high-stakes professions in the world, where it's simply not possible to say "we all make mistakes" when a mistake could literally mean the difference between life and death for a patient. It's a field where perfection is perceived as the standard, and anything less can feel like failure. The hierarchical structure of the medical profession also exacerbates Imposter Syndrome.

The medical field is still navigating systemic gender and racial disparities. Women doctors often face implicit biases, such as being mistaken for nurses or being judged more harshly for mistakes than their male counterparts. Additionally, racial and cultural biases can further marginalize doctors from minority groups, leading them to feel less supported in the workplace.

Medicine demands excellence, resilience, and the ability to remain calm under pressure. For individuals experiencing

Imposter Syndrome, the weight of these expectations can feel unbearable. The pressure to perform flawlessly can also lead to overworking and burnout, regardless of gender, tenure, or seniority.

For those in the medical field, Imposter Syndrome can emerge as early as day one of med school. One study found that a quarter of male and half of female medical students in the US experience Imposter Syndrome, often leading to symptoms of burnout.[9] Not exactly starting their careers off on solid footing. If med students experiencing Imposter Syndrome don't address the root cause, their Imposter Syndrome can follow them all throughout their careers, leading to more overwork, more burnout, and more feeling like a fraud.

And don't think for a second that Imposter Syndrome is only limited to medical doctors and specialists. Dentists, pharmacists, and veterinarians are all prone to the phenomenon.[10] Whenever the stakes are high, which they frequently are in every area of medicine, the pressure can mount, pushing people down the path of Imposter Syndrome.

As Sarah, an emergency physician explains:

> The medical profession attracts high-performing, high-achieving individuals. Simply meeting the criteria for admission to medical school places you among the top echelon of high school students.

Specialist training programs are relentlessly hard, and intensely competitive. By the time you become a specialist in your field, you have undeniably earned your place.

It was surprising and somewhat unsettling, therefore, to reach the position of specialist and feel almost paralyzed by insecurity. I was overwhelmed by the sense that I didn't belong, that my colleagues were all more competent, and that my patients deserved better. This pervasive self-doubt was amplified by the unpredictable and high-stakes nature of emergency medicine, where even your best efforts do not always guarantee a positive outcome.

It was a relief to discover that Imposter Syndrome is a recognized phenomenon that can be addressed and overcome. It was also comforting to realize how widespread it is—that while I was internalizing my own feelings of inadequacy, many of my colleagues were doing the same. These were individuals I admired and respected, people who outwardly seemed as though they had never experienced a moment of self-doubt or questioned their worth. Imposter Syndrome, as it turns out, can affect anyone. Understanding this and employing strategies to overcome it enabled me to find my voice, present myself more confidently, and advocate for my patients more effectively.

### STEM (Science, Technology, Engineering, Math)

In STEM fields, Imposter Syndrome is compounded by systemic biases. Women, minorities, and other underrepresented groups frequently find themselves "the only …" in the room, a phenomenon that creates heightened pressure to prove their worth. This is amplified by persistent stereotypes about who "belongs" in STEM, such as the outdated image of a white, male "genius," which is still often chucked around as the archetype of success in these fields.

Despite progress in diversifying STEM, women and minorities still face implicit bias in hiring, promotions, and opportunities. A 2023 study by the National Science Foundation found that women account for only 35 percent of the STEM workforce in the US and representation for people of color remains disproportionately low.[11] Several factors deter many women from undertaking STEM degrees, including gender stereotypes (engineering is for men!), male-dominated cultures, and fewer role models to inspire and support them.[12] In Australia, women hold only

15 percent of STEM-qualified jobs and at present may earn 17 percent less than men.[13] When women are so underrepresented in STEM fields, it's easy to see why so many feel like they don't belong—they feel like Imposters.

Of course, men studying or working in STEM fields aren't immune to Imposter Syndrome. In fact, they experience Imposter Syndrome just as frequently as women. However, women report lower levels of math self-efficacy, that is, belief in their mathematical ability, which can fuel perfectionism and Imposter thinking.[14]

Imposter Syndrome is particularly prevalent in degrees that are fiercely competitive. That's right—"healthy competition" may not be so healthy for some people. The negative impact of classroom competition has a greater effect on first-generation college students (the first in their families to attend university), an often underrepresented group, fueling Imposter feelings, course disengagement, and dropout. Many first-generation students report attending college for more altruistic reasons than their continuing-generation counterparts, whose motivations are generally more self-serving. Thus, ruthless competition can be at odds with many first-generation students' values.[15] Essentially, they feel out of place, as if they've stepped into a world they're unsuited for, where they believe, or in some instances have been told, they're not welcome.

Imposter Syndrome is prevalent in other underrepresented groups, especially racial minorities when stereotypes and unfair judgment come into play. For example, many Black doctoral and postdoctoral scholars feel they constantly need to prove that they deserve their position. They report that peers often believe their success is the result of affirmative action and it's easier to score a grant if you're a minority.[16] Naturally, when the people around you don't believe you deserve your success, you too can begin to question your achievements.

In STEM fields, the pace of technological innovation and the demand for results, breakthroughs, and funding create a performance-driven culture where mistakes feel catastrophic. Combined with the pressure to constantly prove expertise, individuals often feel they must always deliver exceptional results just to earn a seat at the table. Subtle microaggressions and overt scrutiny are commonplace, contributing to self-doubt and Imposter thinking. For example, a woman engineer might receive more probing questions during a presentation than her male colleagues, leading her to believe she needs to overprepare just to be taken seriously.

These systemic inequities send a subtle message to underrepresented groups: "You're still an outsider here."

### Law

Despite growing numbers of women in law, they're still underrepresented in the legal profession at senior levels. This can lead to feelings of isolation and the pressure to prove themselves in an industry that's still highly male-dominated. However, we are seeing significant shifts; for example, women now make up approximately 41 percent of barristers in Australia, becoming less underrepresented over time.[17]

The legal profession is inherently high-pressure, with significant consequences tied to performance. The weight of responsibility, coupled with the fear of making mistakes, can exacerbate feelings of inadequacy. Additionally, legal work demands precision and perfection, leading to an internalized belief that anything less than flawless performance equates to failure or incompetence.

The constant scrutiny and critical evaluation from peers, judges, and clients can intensify fear and doubt, making individuals question their worth and competence, even when their track record is strong and in circumstances where they have in fact succeeded.

Similar to medicine, the stakes are simply higher in law than in many other fields, as perceived mistakes, displays of vulnerability, and losses can have huge, amplified consequences.

## Banking and Finance

Banking and finance are industries synonymous with competition, high rewards, and intense scrutiny. These fields attract high-achieving individuals, but the relentless focus on results and performance metrics can exacerbate Imposter Syndrome, especially for those who are new to the field or belong to underrepresented groups.

Banking and finance have long been male-dominated sectors, with women and minorities often underrepresented in leadership roles. Even with diversity initiatives, systemic barriers such as the "old boys' club" culture and unconscious biases in mentorship and promotion processes persist. *The Wolf of Wall Street* shone a light on just how this mentality played out in the past. Although times have changed, we see a strong lag from this era still present in parts of the industry.

In finance, the pressure to consistently perform at the top is unrelenting. Whether trying to hit sales targets, deliver client outcomes, or navigate volatile markets, individuals in the industry operate under immense stress. Mistakes, even small ones, can feel career-ending.

In an environment where value is tied to numbers, individuals often feel reduced to their performance metrics and tie their worth and identity purely to success at work. This disconnect between effort and acknowledgment reinforces feelings of inadequacy.

### Executive Assistants and Senior Support Roles

The roles of executive assistants and senior administrators are often misunderstood, with many people assuming that administrative work is menial or simple. These misconceptions can seep into the minds of these highly skilled, high-performing individuals and cast shadows on their achievements and worth. The behind-the-scenes nature of their work means their incredible contributions, visions, execution, innovation, and project management often go unnoticed.

Mistakes can be costly and cause admin professionals to question their abilities and worth. As a result, they may develop perfectionist tendencies fueled by Imposter Syndrome.

Admin professionals regularly find themselves in rooms filled with incredibly accomplished individuals, leaders, innovators, and changemakers. This exposure, while exhilarating, can also fuel feelings of inadequacy despite them earning the right to be in the room, in their role, offering a valuable contribution.

As Candice Burningham, former career senior executive assistant, now founder of Admin Avenues, explains:

> The admin profession, particularly the role of an executive assistant, embodies a unique duality. We are strategic business partners and hands-on problem solvers, balancing sometimes high-stakes

> decision-making with seamless execution. Yet, the constant shifts in priorities, evolving expectations, and the pressure to anticipate needs often create fertile ground for Imposter Syndrome. Despite our vast experience and critical role in driving organizational success, many of us still question our worth. I'm thrilled to see Alison shedding light on this issue because acknowledging and addressing Imposter Syndrome in our profession can unlock further belief in ourselves and even greater confidence and impact in the roles we play.

### Creative, Arts, and Media

Imagine your work being judged by actual critics most of the time. No matter how thick-skinned you are, constant rejection can be very triggering for Imposter Syndrome. Creatives, artists, performers, media stars, whether working or establishing their careers, are often judged subjectively, making it difficult for individuals to measure their success or talent objectively. There's rarely a clear benchmark. Such uncertainty, mixed with highly competitive auditions or job search processes can lead to fear, doubt, and feelings of inadequacy, despite the ability to deliver a confident performance when necessary. The fear of negative feedback on a broad public scale or not living up to expectations can exacerbate Imposter feelings of being exposed.

These industries have also become synonymous with power imbalances, bullying, sexual harassment, and were at the center of the "me too" movement.

As you know now, success is no antidote, even Oscar winners have confessed to crippling bouts of Imposter Syndrome. In these situations, it's important for the individual to create their own healthy definition of competence and success, grounded in self-worth, so it's not all up to the audience or critics, the opinions of which can easily fluctuate day by day, performance by performance, location by location. Social media also plays a huge role in this sector. Seeing the success of peers can fuel feelings of inadequacy, as it can lead to downplaying achievements or individuals feeling that they don't measure up.

Success in creative fields is often inconsistent, with periods of high achievement followed by lulls. This irregularity can make individuals question their abilities during quieter times, contributing to a sense of being undeserving of their past successes.

As actor, comedian, and writer Hannah Sainty explains:

> After years of being away, I threw myself back into the arts and went to England to work with artists I admired. I hadn't performed anything in eight

years and put myself in front of a director who had directed huge films. I'm talking about iconic Hollywood huge. It was a massive deal. At first, I was stoic, trying to force myself into thinking I could do it and that the mere act of trying was enough. *You've done all the work. You're good. You've got this*, I would tell myself. "Fake it till you make it," which I now know wasn't helping. In fact, using the word "fake" was making me feel worse. Then, the night before working with this director, I had the biggest panic attack.

Despite having earned my place in the room, the narrative turned to, *Who the hell are you? Why did you think you could do this? You never "made it" the first time. What makes you think you can do it now? You've had eight years on the bench—and you think you'll somehow be good at it? Like magic? You weren't even good when you were young. What's wrong with you?* I started to hyperventilate and didn't sleep that night.

Hannah's story is all too common in creative industries.

## A SHARED MISSION

While individuals must take ownership of their journey to overcome Imposter Syndrome, organizations and places of work have a responsibility to create supportive environments. By addressing systemic biases, fostering psychological safety, and promoting inclusivity and equity, organizations, institutions, and workplaces can help reduce the triggers and impacts of Imposter Syndrome. With Imposter Syndrome impacting people, culture, innovation, hiring, performance, and profit lines, everybody wins when it's considered in the broader people and culture, leadership, and DEI fabric of the business alongside all other professional and personal development frameworks.

Eradicating Imposter Syndrome in the workplace is a shared mission. Both individuals and organizations have important roles to play, and only through cooperation can we all reap the benefits of a workplace that's free of, or at least sees lower levels of, Imposter Syndrome.

# CHAPTER EIGHT

"When neurodivergence meets Imposter Syndrome, unique brilliance can feel like a burden, and authenticity becomes a constant act of bravery."

—Alison Shamir

# DOUBLE MASKING

## IMPOSTER SYNDROME AND NEURODIVERSITY—IT'S MORE COMMON THAN YOU MIGHT THINK

Imagine Imposter Syndrome being experienced by an individual who is already in some ways "masking" their identity and knows they're in the minority. With approximately 20 percent of individuals identifying as neurodivergent and Imposter Syndrome impacting 70 percent of the population, the overlap creates a significant and often unseen and unexpressed challenge.[1] It can become a "double masking" experience, which is a heavy weight to bear. To quote Sam, someone who experiences Imposter Syndrome and was diagnosed with ADHD as an adult, "That's when the Imposter shit starts."

For years, Sam worked in high-stress environments, pulling a rabbit out of a hat in the small hours of the morning, inventing new ways of solving problems, finding answers intuitively—and then having to justify them somehow to people who didn't get it.

Sam always felt different. Weird. Alone in the way she received and processed information.

As Sam explains, it's "… that feeling of never quite fitting in, jutting out at a slightly odd angle. Being able to see things that others couldn't see, but only ever being in a room with one or two people who'd understand you and give you the head room. Of course, you come out as feeling like you're a total f*cking fake despite all evidence to the contrary."

When I coach individuals diagnosed with ADHD, every single person says that, after their diagnosis, they felt like they could finally take a deep breath. There was no more hiding, no more "faking it," no more masking. Sometimes, however, a diagnosis can be bittersweet. For many of them, the journey to discovering they had both Imposter Syndrome and ADHD practically took a lifetime. If only they had found out sooner, how different their lives might have been—but better late than never.

As of writing, for the past eighteen months, I've been exploring how Imposter Syndrome impacts neurodivergent individuals, and I've had the privilege of hearing from many who have kindly shared their stories. I've also collaborated—and will continue to collaborate—with neurodiversity specialists, such as clinical psychologist Mariane Power, to expand my knowledge. This is the beginning of my neurodiversity and Imposter Syndrome journey, and although there's always more to explore, I want to share what I've learned so far.

## BROADENING THE LENS OF DEI

When we consider what DEI covers, things like race, gender, and physical disability might immediately spring to mind. However, its scope is much broader than that. DEI also covers neurodiversity, which includes autism, ADHD, dyslexia, Tourette's syndrome, and more, all which exist on a spectrum. Because neurodiversity doesn't always present in obvious ways, it can remain undetected and undiagnosed, creating a negative impact on one's life. When awareness is lacking, it can cause problems in the workplace, as leaders or colleagues of neurodivergent individuals often don't understand how to meet their unique needs.[2] If undiagnosed, the individuals themselves might not know what they require to perform at their best.

In the late 1990s, Australian sociologist Judy Singer helped popularize the term "neurodiversity." It emphasizes that neurological variations should be recognized and respected as part of human diversity.

**Judy Singer is often referred to as the "mother of neurodiversity."**

Singer, who was born in Hungary, is the daughter of a Holocaust survivor. Although initially sent to Auschwitz, her Jewish mother survived the war by working in a German airplane factory. In 1956, when Singer was four years old, she left Hungary with her parents to settle in Australia after a failed revolution in her home country.

As the family attempted to build a new life in a strange and foreign land, Singer's mother began behaving oddly. She seemed to be struggling with the new culture and would frequently melt down. Reflecting on those times, Singer doesn't know if her mother's behavior was due to autism, the trauma of the Holocaust, or a combination of the two.

When her own daughter was diagnosed with Asperger's at age nine, Singer noticed similar behaviors in herself. She struggled to make eye contact with others and would often speak in a monotone. Her realization put her on the path to exploring neurodiversity further and eventually writing the 1998 honors thesis that utilized the term.[3]

When Singer helped introduce the concept of neurodiversity to the wider world, she wasn't just trying to popularize an umbrella term for all neurodevelopmental conditions. Her aim was to create a movement—and she succeeded. Judy's work was instrumental in shifting the collective perspective on neurological differences from a deficit-based model to a diversity model. She saw neurological differences as part of the broader spectrum of human diversity rather than pathologies to be cured.[4]

Singer's own personal experiences with neurodiversity gave her a unique perspective on how society views neurological differences. Her work was groundbreaking in framing these differences in a new way, likening them to other forms of diversity, such as gender, race, and sexual orientation. She advocated for societal acceptance and accommodation of neurological variations, emphasizing that neurodivergent individuals should not be seen as defective but as possessing unique strengths and abilities.[5]

Singer's concept of neurodiversity has since gained global traction, particularly within the autism advocacy community, and covers a range of other conditions such as dyslexia, dyspraxia, and dysgraphia. Her contribution has been pivotal in reshaping how society understands neurological conditions, influencing both advocacy movements and clinical approaches around the world.

While Judy Singer's contributions were influential, the idea of recognizing the value of neurological diversity was being explored by other advocates and researchers at around the same time. For example, American journalist Harvey Blume also helped popularize the term in his work, contributing to its widespread acceptance.[6] Clearly, the time was right to promote a new understanding of neurological diversity and create positive change.

Globally, it's estimated that 15–20 percent of people are neurodivergent, with similar rates reported in Australia, the US, and the UK.[7] These aren't insignificant numbers, and it's inevitable that neurodiversity and Imposter Syndrome will have some overlap.

* * *

## THE WEIGHT OF THE DOUBLE MASK

Neurodivergent individuals sometimes assume it must be their fault if other people don't get them because their brains work differently. But it's not their fault, neither is their Imposter experience.

The term "masking" in the context of neurodivergent individuals refers to the conscious or unconscious effort to hide or suppress behaviors, traits, or thought patterns that are associated with their neurodivergence in order to "blend in" with neurotypical people or meet societal expectations. Masking can involve mimicking behaviors, using scripted responses, or adopting mannerisms that are considered socially acceptable to avoid misunderstanding, judgment, or discrimination.

For example:

- Some autistic individuals may mask by forcing themselves to maintain eye contact, suppressing stimming (repetitive movements), or imitating social behaviors they observe in neurotypical peers.
- Some Individuals with ADHD might hide their impulsivity or restlessness by engaging in overpreparation or hyperfocusing on tasks to appear more controlled.

While masking may help neurodivergent individuals navigate social or professional environments, it often comes at a significant emotional and mental cost. Constantly suppressing one's true self can lead to exhaustion, anxiety, and a sense of disconnect from one's identity, contributing to feelings of Imposter Syndrome.

In both Imposter Syndrome and neurodivergence, masking is a defense mechanism driven by fear—fear of judgment, failure, or rejection. For neurodivergent individuals, masking is often about conforming to neurotypical expectations, while for those experiencing Imposter Syndrome, it's about hiding perceived inadequacies or incompetence. The term "double masking" is often used by those who are both neurodivergent and experiencing Imposter Syndrome.

Ultimately, both forms of masking prevent individuals from embracing their authentic selves. Helping neurodivergent individuals and those dealing with Imposter Syndrome to recognize the impact of masking can empower them to step into environments where they feel safe being their true selves.

Ways in which Imposter Syndrome can manifest itself with neurodivergent individuals include but are not limited to:

- **Overcompensation or perfectionism**. Neurodivergent individuals may feel like they have to work harder than neurotypical peers to prove themselves, leading to perfectionist tendencies. Thoughts like, *If I make even one mistake, everyone will know I'm not good enough* are common.

- **Masking and self-comparison**. Many neurodivergent individuals feel the need to mask their traits to fit in with neurotypical norms, which can fuel thoughts like, *I'm only succeeding because I'm hiding my true self* or, *I need to be more like everyone else to be accepted.*

- **Doubting strengths**. Neurodivergent individuals often have strengths that don't fit traditional molds, leading to thoughts like, *My strengths aren't valuable* or, *What I'm good at isn't important.*

- **Fear of exposure**. Thoughts like, *They'll find out I don't actually belong here* or, *I'm just getting by unnoticed* are common, as neurodivergent individuals may fear being judged for processing information differently or needing accommodations.

- **Catastrophizing small mistakes**. A small error may trigger thoughts like, *This one mistake proves I'm a fraud* or, *Everyone will see that I'm incompetent.*

- **Struggling with feedback**. Feedback, even if constructive, can trigger thoughts such as, *I'm not good enough* or, *This shows that I'm not capable*, which can also lead to rejection sensitivity dysphoria.

- **Feeling out of place**: Thoughts like, *I don't belong in this environment* can surface, especially when their way of thinking or working feels different from the majority.

Similarly to neurotypicals, no amount of success allows neurodivergent individuals to "outrun" their Imposter experience. Ultimately, they need to reaffirm to themselves that they belong and that they're worthy, which of course is easier when environments aren't trying to "square peg, round hole" them.

## HIGH ACHIEVERS WITH ADHD AND THEIR COPING STRATEGIES

In the US and Australia, around 1 in 20 people have ADHD.[8] With such high rates, why isn't it more socially acceptable? Several notable people have been open about their ADHD diagnoses, including actor Emma Watson, celebrity chef Jamie Oliver, entrepreneur Bill Gates, actor Ryan Gosling, and Olympic swimmer Michael Phelps.[9] Perhaps the existing stigma comes from a lack of understanding. We're only just starting to fully understand ADHD and what it means for people who have it.

Many adults with ADHD spend a lifetime masking their neurological differences with coping mechanisms. These can include setting multiple alarms for deadlines, taking frequent notes to help remember important tasks, or keeping a detailed calendar. Essentially, they do what they must to succeed in a world that often misunderstands them.

## ADHD IN WOMEN

Another reason why ADHD may go undetected in so many for so long is the fact that ADHD symptoms can vary significantly between men and women. As clinical psychologist and neurodiversity specialist Mariane Power explains:

> The experience of Imposter Phenomenon is particularly pertinent for women who have received a late diagnosis of a brain-based difference, like ADHD or autism. In the absence of a diagnosis, these women (myself included) have spent much of their lives internalizing their struggles as personal flaws, and mislabeling our neurodivergent traits as "lazy" and "incapable." That persistent inner critic that we once believed would propel us toward a potential we knew we were capable of can significantly impact our self-esteem and sense of self-efficacy in ways that produce unnecessary suffering, perpetuate our experience of Imposter Phenomenon

> and stifle our ambitions. An important part of our identity integration is in doing the work to shed the shame that was never ours to own, as we re-author our inner narrative through the lens of neurodiversity.

Terri Martin, former vice chair and non-executive director at ADHD Australia, explains, "Hyperactivity can show up with the inability to sit still, but it can also be hyperactivity in the mind, which often affects women and girls. You're constantly overthinking."

Often, medical professionals misinterpret the symptoms of inattentive ADHD, which can lead to misdiagnosis. They may mistake the condition for anxiety, a mood disorder, or something else entirely.[10] As a result, as clinical psychologist Michelle Frank explains, "There is a lost generation of women who have not been diagnosed ... They hide from their authentic selves and try to fit into a box."[11]

Laetitia Andrac, former strategic consultant and bestselling author of *Light It,* identifies as an Imposter Syndrome sufferer who also has AUDHD—autism and ADHD. While she never tried to hide her differentness, she explains, "For my entire life, I've been thinking differently and behaving differently ... For me, my journey with discovering and embracing diversity was a big permission slip to embracing who I am. Discovering that I was neurodiverse was a moment of, *Ah. That's amazing! I can be who I am.*" However, it took a brush with burnout for her to discover how disease could lead to dis-ease and a breakdown could lead to a breakthrough. Today she is, "Just embracing the wild ride of being a bit different."

## ADHD AND REJECTION-SENSITIVE DYSPHORIA

For many years throughout her career, Laetitia was told she was too emotional. The extreme emotional pain linked to feelings of rejection and shame, often referred to as rejection sensitive dysphoria (RSD), commonly affects children and adults with ADHD.[12]

While RSD isn't an officially recognized diagnosis, many health practitioners and sufferers are well aware of its impact. Triggers for RSD include rejection (whether real or perceived), teasing, criticism (even constructive), and failure (whether real or perceived). The level of distress felt by an individual suffering from RSD depends on the perceived weight of the trigger.[13]

While the exact reason why people with ADHD often experience RSD is unknown, sufferers have provided some insights. Some believe it's a learned response to rejection, exacerbated by difficulties with communication and navigating social norms. Others suggest that people with ADHD are more sensitive to social queues and the signs (or perceived signs) of rejection. For some, the key to overcoming RSD is strong social support.[14]

As Laetitia explains, similarly to Imposter Syndrome, "The condition often triggers a profound and wide-reaching sense of failure, as though the person with RSD hasn't measured up to personal or external expectations."

Terri Martin says the condition interferes with people's ability to regulate their emotional responses to rejection. "This is huge for Imposter Syndrome sufferers … They hang on to any of the negativity that they are told and amplify it way beyond what is necessary. Feelings of not being good enough then get parked on top of that."

Hearing from incredibly talented and competent women like Laetitia, Terri, Mariane and Sam (plus many other incredible individuals) highlights that the overlap between Imposter Syndrome and neurodiversity can no longer be ignored. But it's important to note that not every neurodivergent individual will experience Imposter Syndrome. I've personally spoken to many who don't. Whether you identify as neurodivergent or neurotypical, the first step to overcoming Imposter Syndrome remains the same: owning who you are and taking control of your story. It's time to show the world who you are and remove any "masks" that are holding you back. It's also time for the world to change and clear the runway for your brilliance. Neurodiversity must be a part of any organization's or institution's broader DEI strategy.

A "Diversity in Tech Report" from Tech Talent Charter found that while 50 percent of tech employees identify as neurodiverse, employers believe the number to be only around 3 percent. That's a huge gap between perception and reality. The misconception is due to several factors. For instance, only 68 percent of employers measure neurodiversity among their staff. Even for those that do measure, gathering accurate data can be difficult, as only 69 percent of neurodivergent men and 50 percent of neurodivergent women inform their managers about their situation, which highlights the importance of building trust with employees and providing a supportive environment.[15]

I've had the pleasure to speak to and work with organizations globally that are leading the charge, organizations that have already set up neurodiversity ERGs or BRGs (employee or business resource groups) internally to foster a true culture of inclusion.

There are huge advantages to overcoming Imposter Syndrome and working in a neuroinclusive environment.

For example, inclusion in general can lead to 87 percent better decision-making and generate higher innovation-related revenue—which is nothing to scoff at.[16] Neurodivergent individuals often think differently and therefore see the world and the problems they're trying to solve differently. They bring a fresh and often innovative perspective.

Of course, to truly shine, neurodivergent individuals must feel comfortable and supported in their environments. They must feel they have the freedom to fully express themselves and explore novel solutions to difficult problems. When organizations neglect neuroinclusivity, they not only undermine their bottom line but also one of their greatest assets—their people. If you're neurodivergent, your environment matters. Is it supportive? Or is it holding you back? Of course, switching environments (for example, changing jobs) isn't always easy or even an option. However, awareness and understanding go a long way, especially when it comes to overcoming Imposter Syndrome.

As neurodiversity becomes better-understood, I look forward to seeing where these conversations go and supporting organizations to embrace and empower their neurodivergent talent, while conquering Imposter experiences.

# CHAPTER NINE

"Imposter Syndrome doesn't just impact mental, physical, and emotional health; it can impact our financial health too. There is a cost to prolonged Imposter Syndrome. We all pay a price."

—Alison Shamir

# IMPOSTER IMPACT

## THE INTERCONNECTEDNESS OF IMPOSTER SYNDROME, MENTAL HEALTH, AND MENTAL ILLNESS

When I broke down in the office bathroom on that lonely frightening day in 2013, I felt the true wrath of Imposter Syndrome—and none of it was good.

I was suffering from "high-functioning anxiety," which is common for people with Imposter Syndrome. While high-functioning anxiety isn't included in the DSM (*Diagnostic and Statistical Manual of Mental Disorders*), usually being diagnosed as a general anxiety disorder, it is recognized by many mental health experts. Sufferers are generally high achievers who are good at covering their symptoms, which means their anxiety often goes unnoticed and undiagnosed. On the outside, it looks like they have their shit together, but on the inside it's a different story. They're living in near-constant fear of criticism and appearing foolish or incompetent.[1] Sound familiar? The link between high-functioning anxiety and Imposter Syndrome couldn't be clearer.

Imposter Syndrome is interconnected with both mental health and mental illness, two terms often used interchangeably, yet they have very different meanings.

Mental health refers to a person's overall emotional, psychological, and social wellbeing. It affects how individuals think, feel, and behave in their daily lives, as well as how they handle stress, relate to others, and make decisions. It's a spectrum of emotional and psychological wellbeing that everyone experiences. Mental illness, on the other hand, is a diagnosable condition that significantly disrupts a person's thinking, emotions, behavior, or ability to function in daily life. It may require medical or therapeutic intervention. Highlighting the distinction between the two helps people understand that while maintaining mental health is for everyone, mental illness refers to specific conditions for which some form of treatment is recommended.

Understanding how Imposter Syndrome interconnects with other conditions is important in overcoming it. For example, if you're an individual who has been diagnosed with depression or a depressive disorder, it's almost certainly impacting your experience with Imposter Syndrome. I always recommend addressing the clinical elements of your mental state with appropriate health practitioners first before tackling your Imposter experience.

As a coach, I've witnessed the impacts of Imposter Syndrome on the individuals I coach, as well as thousands of stories from individuals who have approached me after speaking events, networking events, via direct message, interviews, media, and through other avenues. Impacts include:

- **Chronic stress.** Experiencing chronic stress related to their constant need to prove themselves and avoid being "exposed."
- **Burnout.** Burning out from overwork, overwhelm, and exhaustion.
- **Anxiety.** Experiencing anxiety in its many forms, including extreme episodes like panic attacks, regularly.
- **Depression.** Having an existing clinical diagnosis or developing feelings of depression as the weight of their experience grows heavy.
- **Addiction.** Turning to alcohol and other substances as a coping mechanism, or to keep themselves awake to work more, or to come down from high bouts of stress and anxiety.
- **Losing their voice (figuratively).** Not speaking up, sharing their ideas, or advocating for themselves.
- **Risk aversion.** Being held back by catastrophic thoughts and fear of being exposed.

- **Missed opportunities.** Not pursuing opportunities and therefore not reaching their full potential.

- **Identity crises.** Tying their worth to their careers and not knowing who they are anymore after a change in circumstances.

## PHYSICAL MANIFESTATIONS OF IMPOSTER SYNDROME

The effects of Imposter Syndrome aren't just mental. The phenomenon can also cause physical symptoms. We know that battling Imposter Syndrome is a stressful experience, and chronic stress can manifest as fatigue, sleep disorders, and migraines. Often, the physical signs alert us that something is misaligned mentally. When our bodies try to tell us something, it's wise to listen.

For some, the physical and mental symptoms of Imposter Syndrome eventually lead to clinical burnout. The World Health Organization classes burnout as an "occupational phenomenon," not a medical condition.[2] Some consider it a worldwide epidemic.

One study found a strong association between Imposter Syndrome and symptoms of burnout, including physical and emotional exhaustion, cynicism, and depersonalization, in medical students.[3] It's an all-too-common outcome across a variety of roles, careers, and industry sectors. We feel disconnected, defeated, and sometimes depressed.

Generally, those of us who experience Imposter Syndrome are high performers—even if we don't see it that way. We usually spend a lot of time outside of our comfort zones, often with ambitious goals and demanding careers. We're driven to succeed. We frequently push boundaries, and ourselves, to achieve that success. However, as high achievers experiencing Imposter Syndrome, we can become so used to pushing ourselves that we ignore the bodily signals that are trying to tell us that something is wrong, but we can only ignore the warning signs for so long before—*bam!*—burnout hits like a ton of bricks. If you're experiencing symptoms of burnout, which could include exhaustion, irritability, anger, chronic stress, brain fog, sleep disturbances, or emotional fragility, ask yourself, *Is Imposter Syndrome to blame?*

Several studies have confirmed the connection between Imposter Syndrome and burnout. One 2022 study, which focused on mental health professionals, found that Imposter Syndrome is not only a good predictor of burnout but also compassion fatigue, a type of burnout that affects caregivers who assist traumatized individuals. Due to the pressures of the job, mental health professionals, even experienced therapists, can face crippling self-doubt and feelings of inadequacy, which can of course lead to Imposter Syndrome.[4] Another 2022 study, which focused on resident physicians, tells a similar story. Imposter Syndrome is fuel for both anxiety and burnout, which is crucial information for an industry where burnout is prevalent.[5] For many professionals across multiple industries, the struggle is real.

I used to be ashamed to admit this, but I've been clinically burned out twice in my life. Well, actually, three times, but I'm still in denial about burnout number three. My first burnout occurred in 2013 when I suffered that debilitating panic attack caused by months of prolonged Imposter-Syndrome-induced anxiety.

My second brush with burnout occurred at the end of 2019 when I was ten months into business ownership. This time, Imposter Syndrome wasn't to blame—we had been broken up for years. So, who or what was the culprit? Well, because I'm a high-performing high achiever, I naturally threw myself into my business headfirst and without restraint, working around the clock, struggling to find balance. Essentially, I left my corporate 8 a.m. to 6 p.m. gig to work 24/7, losing control and careening down the path to burnout.

Workaholism is common among high-achieving professionals. High-performing individuals often struggle to disengage from work, and even when they're not technically working, their minds may be stuck in the office or business venture.[6] We know that Imposter Syndrome can lead to overworking, but not every workaholic feels like a fraud. Stress is another contributing factor, which of course is naturally higher in high-pressure roles—the types of roles that high achievers generally gravitate toward.[7]

So, what did burnout number two look like for me? One afternoon, I was standing in my kitchen making a cup of coffee, my fifth or sixth of the day, and as I stirred my drink the strangest sensation came over me. It felt like there were tabs open in my brain and they were clicking shut one by one. I felt each little "click"; then my vision went blurry; my blood pressure dropped, and I thought, *I'm going to faint, I'm going to faint,* so I dropped to the kitchen floor and just lay there. I couldn't get up; the room was spinning. Mustering all my strength and focus, I crawled around the corner and into the living room, made it to the lounge, and there I lay, alone, with blurry vision, absolutely exhausted.

It's like my brain ran an intercept and announced, "Alison, I'm shutting you down!" It took me four days to feel even remotely like myself again. I couldn't work; I couldn't focus; all I needed was rest, and I was fortunate that my partner provided wonderful support. It was another stark reminder of the power of the brain and body, how our brains are inherently designed to keep us alive, protect us, and keep us moving safely from harm. It was a huge wake-up call. Unfortunately, as I mentioned, it wasn't my final burnout experience.

The third time was in 2022. However, this episode happened only four months after the passing of my father. I was in the midst of intense grief, yet at the same time driving myself hard. Luckily, a trip to the US provided a circuit breaker and some much-needed rest and recovery, especially when I reached the aloha state.

## COMPETENCY TYPES AND THE BURNOUT CONNECTION

When it comes to Imposter Syndrome, in my experience, burnout is particularly common among, but not restricted to, certain Imposter competency types—the perfectionist, the superhuman, and the expert. First coined by Dr. Valerie Young, these definitions provide insight into the underlying traits that can fuel the type of overwork that can lead to burnout. While we discussed all five competency types in chapter six, we'll now focus on the three most closely connected to burnout that I've witnessed and the experiences of some high-performing, high-achieving individuals who have come through the Conquer Your Imposter™ program.

- **The perfectionist** fixates on every detail and sets unrealistic expectations for themselves. They also procrastinate heavily due to fear of failure and *it not being perfect.* Then they move to action under tight deadlines and experience extreme stress. This often yields results, but they discount them anyway. Thus is the self-sabotaging nature of perfectionism. They're never satisfied. I remember this well, and, in fact, my own perfectionist tendencies were triggered by writing this book. Not by my Imposter Syndrome, which is long gone, but because I can still at times fixate on details. Fortunately, I've learned to intercept and redirect this behavior so I can move forward.

- **The superhuman** juggles multiple tasks, wears many hats (often simultaneously), and needs to do it all at a high level. In my experience, they're often excessive people pleasers and find it difficult to switch off, set boundaries, or say no out of fear of being perceived as incompetent or less than. Any missed task or need to delegate is considered a weakness to those who align with superhuman views. This isn't to be mistaken for individuals who love to and can handle juggling multiple tasks and actions. I do have some clients who prefer this, which is fine as long as they're taking adequate breaks and have established clear boundaries so their juggling act serves them, not sabotages them. When it doesn't serve us, we know we're pushing back on Imposter Syndrome.

- **The expert** is driven by a need to accumulate knowledge. More qualifications, more certifications, more experience, more this, more that—it's all about quantity. It's a relentless pursuit of knowledge where they simultaneously seek to "outrun" their Imposter feelings. It's also a one-way ticket to burnout. When working with clients who align with the expert view on competence, I bring their attention quickly back to the story underpinning this behavior. Although they're ambitious, it's the Imposter fear that's in the driver's seat, which means no matter what they accumulate or achieve, they'll discount it anyway. We need to break this cycle.

Another commonality among my clients and many who experience Imposter Syndrome is, when they're driving themselves to these unrelenting and self-sabotaging standards, they're often surrounded by other people, yet they feel so isolated. They feel like they're the only ones struggling. This loneliness can be compounded by a reluctance to share these feelings out of fear of judgment or rejection. Many individuals with Imposter Syndrome feel ashamed of their perceived inadequacies or guilty for "deceiving" others into thinking they're competent. These emotions create a heavy emotional burden that can be difficult to shake.

As we know, Imposter Syndrome can trigger a host of stressors and mental health conditions. For example, individuals with Imposter Syndrome experience high levels of work-related depression and anxiety.[8] If they don't address the problem head-on, which of course involves conquering Imposter Syndrome, the negative effects can compound over time. The result? Burning out, often in a big way.

## A RECIPE FOR SOCIAL ANXIETY

Throughout the COVID-19 pandemic, on top of typical burnout, we also saw the rise of lockdown fatigue and "languishing," a feeling of joylessness, aimlessness, and emptiness.[9] As a society, many of us were thoroughly exhausted, and social anxiety, usually more prevalent in younger generations, impacted people across senior ranks, as we were all forced behind screens.

While, in the aftermath of COVID, flexible work arrangements have made life easier for some by reducing time spent commuting and granting better work-life balance, there are some downsides. When we spend less time interacting with people face-to-face, we can become more socially anxious when the time comes for an in-person meeting or discussion. We're simply not used to those types of interactions. If someone is new to the workforce and remote work is their only experience, in-person interactions can feel even more daunting.

Naturally, Imposter Syndrome can compound any social anxiety an individual already has. Not only are they anxious about interactions in general, but they're terrified of being outed as a fraud. Imagine feeling like every conversation is an interrogation where you must convince the other person you know what you're doing and deserve to be there, even if you don't believe it yourself. Of course you'd be anxious!

Some common triggers of Imposter Syndrome in individuals experiencing social anxiety are:

- Meeting new people.
- Social media and the negative cycle of comparing yourself to others.
- Suddenly being at the table with executive stakeholders who want to hear what you have to say—pressure to perform on the spot.
- Public speaking.
- Teams giving public critiques of your work.
- Being in large groups.

- Not getting enough feedback, which can leave you questioning yourself and ruminating.
- Working from home or isolating conditions where you don't get the cues from body language, which can lead to misinterpreting written messages as negative.

The key to mitigating social anxiety and Imposter Syndrome is firstly to know you're not alone and secondly to recognize the triggers, while utilizing all other tools in this book. If, however, the source of social anxiety runs much deeper, you may need to explore your experience with an appropriate health practitioner.

## THE FINANCIAL BURDEN OF IMPOSTER SYNDROME

If left unchecked, Imposter Syndrome can cost you more than just your mental and physical wellbeing. It can also cost you money—that's right, I'm talking about cold, hard cash. The financial repercussions of Imposter Syndrome are easy to overlook, as they aren't always obvious, especially if you're unaware of the connection.

Imposter Syndrome can cost you money by preventing you from:

- Negotiating your worth in a salary review or job interview.

- Putting your hand up for an internal promotion or position with a new company.
- Launching your own business.
- Increasing your existing rates or fees.
- Creating financial independence by investing your money or through other means.

The financial impacts can compound greatly across your life and career. Imposter Syndrome holds you back from new and lucrative opportunities, which, unsurprisingly, can negatively impact your earning potential. Missed promotions or opportunities for growth mean you're not advancing as quickly as you could be, which has a cumulative effect on your financial position. When your Imposter story is firing, you can undervalue yourself, which makes selling yourself to others a near-impossible task, leading to a lower negotiated salary and missed opportunities for career progression. Women are particularly susceptible to the financial repercussions of Imposter Syndrome. Author and researcher Clare Josa's 2019 Imposter Syndrome study found that 37 percent of women in the UK, in the year leading up to the survey, had not asked for a pay rise they knew they had earned.[10] That's a huge amount of money potentially left on the table.

When opportunities present themselves, you may think:

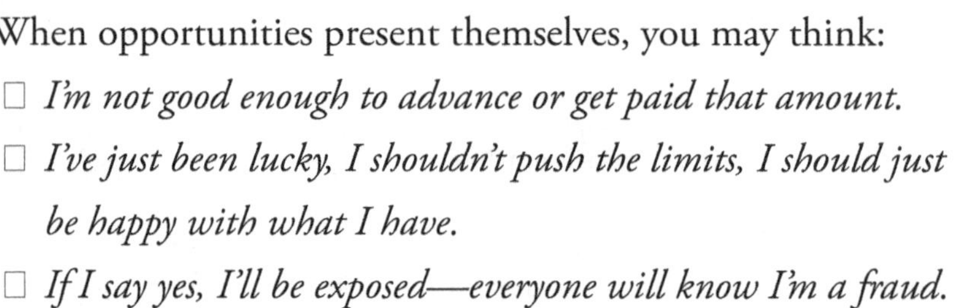

- ☐ *I'm not good enough to advance or get paid that amount.*
- ☐ *I've just been lucky, I shouldn't push the limits, I should just be happy with what I have.*
- ☐ *If I say yes, I'll be exposed—everyone will know I'm a fraud.*

In these situations, we may also see the Imposter Syndrome hallmark of *fear of success* raise its head. It might seem counterintuitive because we assume that everyone wants to succeed. However, the fear of success is a complex psychological phenomenon that can coexist with Imposter Syndrome for several reasons:

- **Increased expectations.** When someone with Imposter Syndrome achieves success, it often leads to heightened expectations from others. This can create pressure to consistently perform at a high level, causing fear that they won't be able to meet these new expectations. This fear can be paralyzing and lead them to avoid situations where they might succeed, which also has financial impacts.

- **Visibility.** Success can bring increased visibility and attention, which can be uncomfortable for individuals with Imposter Syndrome. They may fear the scrutiny and judgment that can come with success, worrying that others will discover their perceived inadequacies.

- **Attribution of success.** People with Imposter Syndrome tend to attribute their successes to external factors, like luck or help from others, rather than recognizing their own abilities. When success occurs, they may worry that they won't be able to repeat it, leading to self-doubt and anxiety about future performance, rather than owning the current success and performing at their best. I touched on this briefly with the Sylvester Stallone story.

- **Impending failure.** Paradoxically, the fear of success can also be rooted in the anticipation of failure. When someone with Imposter Syndrome achieves success, they may worry that their next endeavor will inevitably result in failure, reinforcing their sense of being a fraud.

- **Change and the unknown.** Success often leads to change, whether it's in the form of increased responsibilities, new challenges, or a shift in one's identity. People with Imposter Syndrome may fear the unknown and be uncomfortable with change, even if it's positive.

This cycle of negative thinking (automatic negative thoughts, or ANTs) can leave you stuck in place, unable to make the decisions and take the actions necessary to improve your situation and reach the success you deserve—because you believe you *don't* deserve it. You're still a high performer, but you're not internalizing or enjoying your success. When we're paralyzed by Imposter Syndrome, many of us don't act toward what we want, leading to missed opportunities and feeling even worse. It's easy to see how we can get stuck in that vicious cycle ... which is why I recommend you now reexamine the questions asked in chapter three:

- How do you define success and competence?
- How are these definitions making you behave?
- What is the cost of these behaviors, mentally, physically, emotionally, financially?
- Do you believe you're serving yourself through these behaviors or sabotaging yourself?

## IMPOSTER IMPACT BEYOND THE INDIVIDUAL

As we know from our discussion in chapter seven around Imposterization™ (the impact of workplaces on Imposter Syndrome), Imposter Syndrome can negatively affect teams and flow through entire organizations.

For example, perfectionist tendencies can hinder productivity and, in a leader, can lead to excessive micromanagement, causing stress for team members. Procrastinating and paralysis due to a lack of belief in ourselves and our abilities can prevent us from completing any meaningful work—we feel unable to act. We may also experience people-pleasing tendencies, which can lead to stress and overwork.[11] Overworking tendencies can then spiral into failing to set boundaries, meaning we're often giving more than we're being paid for, creating an imbalance that affects both our financial and emotional wellbeing.

For organizations, the implications are *massive*. How can teams be consistently effective when the majority (approximately 70 percent) of people, which can include the leaders, are questioning their worth and fear being found out to be not good enough? The answer—it's very difficult. As touched on in chapter seven, Imposter Syndrome impacts health and wellbeing, performance, communication, and culture, which can detrimentally impact creativity, innovation, collaboration, and profit lines. This is why it's crucial that Imposter Syndrome and its intersectionality is understood across any people, performance, and culture strategies, programs, and initiatives and it is also hugely advantageous when included in any overarching DEI planning, policies, and commitments.

For as long as Imposter Syndrome skews our belief in ourselves and our perceptions of competence, it will influence how we show up in the world and block us from recognizing our true worth and accomplishments. Recognizing the personal toll it can take on us is a key step toward change.

We high-performing high achievers are great at ignoring signals and wearing "masks" when in the midst of Imposter Syndrome. The good news is that the impacts aren't permanent. With awareness, strategies, and support, you can break free. It's time to remove the mask.

# CHAPTER TEN

"The difference between someone experiencing Imposter Syndrome and someone who isn't is not their intelligence, talent, or skills; it's the story they tell themselves."

—Alison Shamir

# CONQUER YOUR IMPOSTER™

## IT WON'T BE EASY ... BUT IT WILL BE WORTH IT

Success isn't easy. It demands discipline, patience, and a relentless dedication to your goals. Writing this book, I'm reminded of a truth I've lived and now share with audiences worldwide: the journey to success and self-mastery, however you choose you to define it, isn't linear or effortless, but it's absolutely worth it. True success is when you can internalize it, know you've earned it, and celebrate it. It's when you thrive, not just survive. Imposter Syndrome will block your ability to recognize your success and therefore your ability to authentically thrive, which is why it's important to apply the same discipline, patience, and relentless dedication to understanding your journey with the phenomenon, learning to navigate and ultimately conquer it. It's the same approach you would take to achieve anything big in your life or career.

The journey to conquer Imposter Syndrome isn't meant to be easy. If it were easy, the phenomenon would be a thing of the past. But I know you're committed to the cause, because you're here.

## WHAT DOES IT MEAN TO CONQUER IMPOSTER SYNDROME?

The word *conquer* originates from the Latin word *conquirere*, meaning "to seek or gain," and evolved into the Old French *conquerre*, meaning "to overcome or subdue." Over time, its meaning has expanded to reflect the act of achieving victory, whether over an external adversary, a personal challenge, or a set of internal barriers. At its core, *to conquer* means to triumph over adversity or a challenge. It involves confronting something difficult or intimidating and emerging victorious.

In the context of Imposter Syndrome, this reflects the ability to face limiting beliefs, negative stories, and self-doubt despite evidence of competence and ability, and break the self-sabotaging behavioral patterns driven by these challenges. It's about taking back control of what you can, taking ownership of what you've achieved, recognizing your worth and the fact that it's not tied to achievements, and unlocking your true potential, thus far inhibited by your Imposter experience.

In chapter one, I mentioned that 30 percent of people never experience Imposter Syndrome. They carry the titles of neuroscientist, marketing director, CEO, board member, head of HR, management consultant, brand manager, entrepreneur, professional athlete, and surgeon to name a few. What do these individuals have in common? They tell themselves very different stories. Their stories aren't free of self-doubt or fears (we all have those), but they don't question their worth. They've developed healthy views of competence and success, have ensured what they "do" doesn't define their whole identity, and are aware that chasing "perfection" in terms of how they measure their own competence is, in fact, a huge barrier to success if its driven by fear and leads to self-sabotage. They've also developed realistic responses to criticism, mistakes, and failure. They're committed to testing and learning, to ongoing growth while acknowledging and internalizing milestones and achievements gained or reached. They're high-achieving high performers, but they don't battle Imposter Syndrome—and you don't have to continue to battle it either.

The story we tell ourselves is the foundation of how we see the world, and how we see ourselves within it. For those experiencing Imposter Syndrome, this story often takes the form of a relentless narrative of inadequacy, fear, and self-doubt. It whispers that you're not enough, that you don't belong, and that your achievements are somehow fraudulent. This story is not only false, but it also robs you of the joy, true confidence, and freedom you deserve.

But here's the truth: *You're not bound to the story you've been telling yourself.* You have the power to rewrite it, to redirect the narrative, and to create a story that's grounded in your worth, your identity, and your accomplishments. This isn't about surface-level affirmations or looking in the mirror and saying, "I'm good enough." It's about going deep, connecting with the undeniable evidence of your success and allowing that evidence to guide you toward a new, authentic identity, free of Imposter Syndrome.

After more than a decade working with Imposter Syndrome sufferers, coaching hundreds of high-performing high achievers, each influenced by diverse cultural, behavioral, and environmental factors, I've developed the proprietary Conquer Your Imposter™ coaching framework, consisting of three key pillars—*Identify, Intercept, and Redirect*™. Each pillar contains three levels, which means there are nine stages to understanding, navigating, and conquering Imposter Syndrome.

- **Identify** explores such factors as the root causes of your Imposter Syndrome, including your origin story and triggers.

- **Intercept** explores such factors as intercepting the automatic negative thoughts (ANTs), skewed perceptions of competence, and self-sabotaging behaviors fueled by your stories and thoughts.

- **Redirect** explores such factors as defining a new evidence-based narrative that supports your self-worth, acknowledgment of accomplishments, and new self-serving actions to replace the self-sabotage.

## TAKE CONTROL OF YOUR STORY

The most critical step in overcoming Imposter Syndrome is to take control of the story you tell yourself. This can also be the most challenging step for many high performers, as they prefer to focus on the other actions. In fact, many clients I've worked with would rather do a million other actions than tackle this one, because it can be confronting. We can be in denial about the fact that this negative story has been ruling our lives. This is the benefit of working with an expert coach—we already have the experience, tools, case studies, and platforms, and we can guide you through every step. But when it comes to conquering Imposter Syndrome, it's not just the steps you take; it's the order in which you take them that ensures you make meaningful, measurable, and lasting change.

We need to move from your Imposter story, driven by self-deprecating and untrue language, to a new true story grounded in evidence that reaffirms self-belief and self-mastery. This isn't toxic positivity or "woo-woo"; it's science.

Your new story is your "evidence-based statement." Here's how it works:

- **Identify the old story.** Reflect on the narrative you've been telling yourself. What are the recurring themes? Perhaps it's "I'm not smart enough," "I'm just lucky," or "I'll never be as good as them." Write these down to bring them into the light.

- **Redirect the story.** Using the evidence available to you (evidence you've long been ignoring like current success, results, awards, experience, feedback, and so on), craft a new true narrative that reflects your strengths, accomplishments, and potential anchored in self-worth first.

  Here's an example:

  ***I'll never be as good as them*** can be redirected to …

*I have unique strengths, and I belong in this room. Any other knowledge or skills can be acquired as I go.*

*I deserve to be here and have nothing to prove. I'll do the best I can and seek help when I need it.*

*My voice matters, and I have valuable information to contribute. I'll share my views and seek feedback as needed.*

- **Reinforce the new story.** Repeat this new narrative to yourself, not as a passive mantra but as an active intentional reminder of your truth. This is the science of self-talk in action.

This process is transformative because it reconnects you with your self-worth, allowing you to step forward as your most authentic and confident self regardless of how you gender identify. If I hadn't let go of the story I held, perpetrated by my own mother, I would have been destined to feel not good enough or not worthy enough, regardless of how successful I became. That's if I had become successful at all.

Did I experience environmental triggers, such as workplace toxicity, bully bosses, and harassment? Yes, they exacerbated my Imposter feelings, but I couldn't control those things. I could only control myself. As discussed in chapter seven—do negative environments, systems, and structures need to change? Yes. Will they change faster than you can change your own conscious choices and actions? Probably not. So, I always recommend starting by focusing on what you can control, which then stands you in good stead if you want to contribute to tackling environmental circumstances later down the track.

When it comes to adult learning, control the controllables first, and practice makes progress due to plasticity.[1] It's time to learn a new and better way of operating. We must move beyond your Imposter story and into the realm of self-belief mastery.

---

*"It doesn't matter who you are, where you come from.*
*The ability to triumph begins with you. Always."*
*—Oprah*

---

As I advance clients through the Conquer Your Imposter™ program, just as I've advanced you through these chapters, we transition to the 4R Framework™ (nicknamed "pirate" by a client, because of all the RRRRs, get it?).

> "*Redirect*, ***Reaffirm***, Reward, **Repeat.**"

## BREAKING SELF-SABOTAGING HABITS WITH THE 4R FRAMEWORK™

To sustain your transformation, you must address the habits that have kept you stuck in the cycle of Imposter Syndrome. These habits—like procrastination, perfectionism, or overworking—aren't just behaviors; they're deeply ingrained patterns rooted in fear and self-protection. Breaking them requires understanding how habits work and using neuroscience-backed strategies to create new, supportive, and self-serving behaviors.

*Redirect* signifies new action. We're redirecting an old self-sabotaging behavior and replacing it with a new self-serving action. With enough repetition, it will cement as a new habit, thus breaking the automatic negative cycles driven by Imposter Syndrome.

*Reaffirm* signifies our acknowledgment of the step taken and the success or result achieved. We must acknowledge it in order to teach the brain that this was a new and "good" action. For this, I want you to talk to yourself—yes, that's right—aka self-validation. This step is crucial when conquering Imposter Syndrome because, as we know, it's driven by the story you tell yourself, and that story blocks your ability to truly internalize your success and accomplishments.

Finally, *reward* and *repeat* cement the formation of new self-serving habits.

When you utilize the 4R Framework™, you begin to form the habits that will ultimately lead to conquering Imposter Syndrome for good.

## THE SCIENCE OF HABIT FORMATION AND CHANGE

Habits are formed through a three-step process: cue, routine, reward. This loop governs how behaviors are triggered and reinforced.

- **Cue.** A trigger that initiates the behavior (for example, a looming deadline).

- **Routine.** The behavior itself (for example, overworking, avoiding tasks, or ruminating).

- **Reward.** The perceived benefit of the behavior (for example, temporary relief from anxiety or fear).

To break self-sabotaging habits, you must disrupt this loop with new intentional actions. The key first step is to recognize the triggers. What's triggering the self-sabotaging habit (what, where, when)? Once you identify the trigger, you must then replace the self-sabotaging habit with one that's self-serving.[2] For example, if receiving criticism (what) at work (where) triggers Imposter thoughts that then lead to overworking, edging you ever closer to burnout, you've found your trigger—criticism. So, instead of letting the negative story emerge and overworking yourself, you can choose a more self-serving action as a replacement, such as accepting valid criticism as an opportunity to grow or, if the criticism isn't constructive, using evidence-based statements to remind yourself of your ability and worth. Over time, if you repeat the new action, it will eventually become a habit.[3]

## THE POWER OF REWARDS IN HABIT FORMATION

Rewards are a critical component of habit formation because they signal to the brain that a behavior is beneficial and worth repeating. When we reward ourselves for taking positive action, whether it's completing a challenging task or simply recognizing our own efforts, we trigger the release of dopamine, a neurotransmitter associated with pleasure and motivation. The first and easiest way to reward ourselves when conquering Imposter Syndrome is with *reaffirmation.* It's available immediately. After reaffirming themselves by acknowledging the great step they just took, some clients choose to extend the reward into things like an hour off work, the purchase of an object or experience, eating their favorite meal, a walk in the sun, or something else they enjoy. All of these rewards bring them joy, which is important. A reward should feel like and be acknowledged as a reward.

A dopamine release does more than just make us feel good in the moment; it also reinforces the neural pathways associated with the new behavior. In essence, the brain learns to associate the behavior with a sense of accomplishment and satisfaction, making us more likely to repeat it in the future. When overcoming Imposter Syndrome, this means linking new habits, such as speaking to ourselves with evidence-based statements, to a tangible or emotional reward. For example, when you acknowledge your success and remind yourself of the hard work you've done, the positive feedback loop created by dopamine tells your brain, *This is worth doing again.* Over time, these reinforced pathways become stronger, helping you stay in the loop of self-serving habits rather than falling back into cycles of self-sabotage. If you tell yourself you belong in the room or that you're worthy, and repeat this consistently, your brain will believe it.

## THE ROLE OF REPETITION AND NEURAL PATHWAYS

Building new habits isn't a one-time effort; it requires consistent repetition to create lasting change. Conquering Imposter Syndrome isn't a quick fix; it also requires repetition to create lasting change. As adults, our brains are less malleable than those of children, meaning that creating new neural pathways, the physical connections in the brain that drive our behaviors, takes sustained effort and practice. Neuroscience shows that the more we repeat a behavior, the stronger the neural pathway becomes, eventually making the behavior automatic. This process is known as neuroplasticity and allows the brain to reorganize itself and adapt to new patterns of thought and action.

To cement new habits, particularly those that help us redirect self-sabotaging behaviors into confident and self-serving actions, repetition is key. Research suggests it takes an average of 66 days to form a new habit, although this can vary depending on the individual and the complexity of the habit.[4] This is why my Conquer Your Imposter™ coaching program runs for twelve weeks—we need adequate time not just to understand and dismantle your journey with Imposter Syndrome but also to implement, test, and refine the new self-serving actions in your life and environments. During this time, each repetition strengthens the new neural pathway, making it easier to default to the desired behavior over time. For someone overcoming Imposter Syndrome, this means consistently practicing evidence-based statements until they're embedded as new beliefs and redirecting self-sabotage to new self-serving actions. Of course, the approach also involves celebrating small wins.

By consciously repeating positive actions, you rewire your brain to support your growth and success, ultimately replacing the old patterns with empowering habits of success.

## STRIVE FOR EXCELLENCE, NOT PERFECTION

Now ... introducing my 3Es for sustained high performance—excellence, effort, and energy.

- **Excellence** (achieving it) means performing tasks to the best of your ability, not perfectly but exceptionally well. It focuses on outcome quality and impact rather than flawlessness.

- **Effort** is the dedication and hard work put into tasks. It's about the process and the journey toward achieving goals, emphasizing perseverance and resilience.

- **Energy** refers to the mental and physical stamina required to undertake tasks. Managing energy wisely is crucial, as it ensures you can sustain high performance without burnout.

When you learn to identify what's "good enough" to get the task, job, or action done, it's a game changer for your productivity, confidence, and overall satisfaction. Even in the most precision-driven careers, such as in most of the STEM fields, mistakes, delays, failures, and rejection happen. No individual or organization can be flawless, as mistakes and shortcomings are part of the journey.

---

*"This realization is liberating, but only when you've conquered your Imposter Syndrome, because Imposter Syndrome has you fixating on the 1 percent 'mistake' or 'gap' as opposed to celebrating the 99 percent excellence, achievement, or result."*
*—Alison Shamir*

---

So, what is "good enough?" Good enough is a pragmatic approach that prioritizes efficiency and effectiveness. It means delivering work that meets *necessary standards and achieves desired outcomes* without unnecessary time or embellishment. "Good enough" allows for progress in situations where perfection could hinder momentum.

Good enough work is adequately detailed and complete to fulfill its purpose and move projects forward. It's not substandard; rather, it's a strategic decision to optimize time and resources.

Here are some strategies to help you decide when "good enough" is appropriate:

1. **Prioritize tasks.** Identify high-priority tasks where excellence is crucial and lower-priority items where good enough suffices. Delegate where possible and

practice setting small boundaries to protect your time and energy.

2. **Set clear objectives.** Understand the requirements and expectations for each task. If objectives can be met without extra polish, consider it complete.

3. **Consult with stakeholders.** Sometimes, discussing expectations with others can clarify what level of detail and quality is necessary (don't just believe your Imposter voice if it pipes up, run an intercept by speaking to others).

4. **Assess impact.** Evaluate the impact of additional effort. If the incremental benefit is minimal, it might be a sign that the task is already good enough.

Because you don't have infinite energy, save it and your maximum effort for where it's really needed. Not every task requires excellence. Sometimes "good enough" is good enough.

### Excellence vs. Perfection

The pursuit of excellence is about striving to do your best within realistic constraints and structures. It involves continuous improvement, learning from feedback, and adapting processes to enhance quality and efficiency. Unlike Imposter Syndrome induced perfectionism, which is often rigid and static, excellence is dynamic and responsive to change.

Embracing the 3Es—excellence, effort, and energy—will help you recognize when to invest your best and when to opt for good enough. This is only possible when you've redirected your Imposter story. Because when Imposter Syndrome is in the driver's seat, you can't define, let alone be happy with, "good enough."

---

*"By focusing on excellence as a flexible goal rather than an inflexible rule, you can enhance both your performance and your wellbeing."*
*–Alison Shamir*

---

I encourage you to commit to being excellent when it counts and efficient all the time. In this balance lies your greatest chance for success, not just in your role but also in keeping your Imposter feelings at bay (or conquering them entirely).

## THE DELICATE BALANCE BETWEEN CRITIQUE AND CRITICISM

As high performers, the way we evaluate our actions and outcomes significantly impacts our development, self-perception, and success. Critiquing our own performance is a key part of maintaining high performance. We evaluate, question, compliment, and implement change as needed. Or as I say to my clients: we turn the *High Performance Dial*™ as required.

So, what's the difference between critique and criticism?

At its core, critique is a constructive process. It involves analyzing performances and outcomes to identify both strengths and areas for improvement. Constructive critique is rooted in objectivity and growth. It's about recognizing the journey of progress, not just fixating on the destination.

In contrast, criticism, especially when self-directed, often crosses into negative territory, focusing on faults and shortcomings, often irrationally. This negativity can stunt growth, as it shifts the focus from constructive development to self-deprecation and doubt despite evidence of success. Harsh self-criticism fuels Imposter experiences and keeps you in a fear-based state that overshadows your perception of your capabilities.

The key is to identify when healthy self-reflection turns into destructive self-criticism, and practice some self-compassion, which grants a competitive edge when battling Imposter Syndrome.

Self-compassion isn't a sign of weakness; rather, it's a strength. It's about giving yourself the same kindness and understanding you would offer to others. When you practice self-compassion, you create a supportive environment for your growth. It's not about lowering standards, but recognizing and embracing your humanity (remember, strive for excellence, not unhealthy perfection).

Self-critique enables you to bounce back from setbacks, learn from your experiences, and continue pushing forward with resilience and confidence. It's an essential skill for high achievers, but it's vital to ensure that the process is constructive, not destructive. Self-critique should be a tool for growth, not a weapon for self-sabotage. Remember, being kind to yourself doesn't make you "soft" or "weak"; it makes you sustainably powerful.

## THE COMPARISON COIN™

For many individuals, comparison feels like a constant companion driven by their Imposter Syndrome. But what if I told you, *it also has the potential to fuel growth, resilience, and success when used wisely.* Yes, you read that right. The answer lies in how we approach it. So, let's flip the *comparison coin* and explore both sides.

How can we shift from self-sabotage to admiration?

## Comparison as Self-Sabotage

When we compare ourselves to others and immediately feel "less than" or question our worth and belonging, Imposter Syndrome has been triggered. We might think, *Everyone else is smarter than me. Who am I to lead this team? I'll never be worth what that person is paid.* High achievers frequently fall into this trap, measuring their worth against external achievements rather than their own authentic self, strengths, and growth potential. This can stifle progress and if you identified that this is part of your Imposter cycle, we need to break it.

## Comparison as Admiration

On the flip side, when we view others' strengths, actions, or accomplishments through a lens of admiration rather than self-deprecation, comparison becomes empowering. It allows us to look up to those we respect and even adopt their strategies or mindsets, while still remaining our authentic selves. Instead of seeing others' success as something we'll never achieve, we can see it as evidence of what's possible, fueling inspiration and motivation. In this light, comparison becomes a tool for growth rather than a barrier.

Here are some steps to help you move from self-sabotage to admiration:

- **Identify the traits you admire.** When you notice yourself comparing, pause and ask what specifically you admire in that person. Is it their confidence? Their work ethic? Their innovative ideas? This clarity allows you to turn your attention toward developing those traits within yourself and acting on them in *your way*, giving comparison a productive purpose.

- **Recognize your unique strengths.** High achievers and high performers sometimes overlook their own talents in pursuit of what others have. Acknowledge what you bring to the table *first* and how these strengths can complement the qualities you admire in others, not detract from them.

- **Set goals inspired by comparison, not driven by it.** Rather than feeling diminished by someone else's success, use it to set a personal goal that aligns with your growth. This could mean learning to show yourself more self-compassion, reaffirming yourself through self-talk, learning a new skill, building a network, or improving your resilience. When you take this approach, comparison becomes a launchpad for development.

To be clear—this isn't about turning yourself into another person. It's about admiring those who inspire you, learning from them, and applying what you like in ways that are authentic and meaningful for you.

*Being your authentic self is where your power lies.*

Comparison doesn't have to be the thief of joy; it can be the source of it. When we approach it with admiration rather than envy, comparison transforms from a self-sabotaging behavior into a powerful motivator, helping us reach new heights without undermining our self-worth.

## IMPOSTER TO UNSTOPPABLE™ CONFIDENCE

---

*"Careers are a jungle gym, not a ladder."*
*—Sheryl Sandberg*

---

Finally, we've reached the topic of confidence. It's at the back of the book because, as I shared earlier, confidence is just one of the trilogies of self, and it's not the most critical when it comes to understanding, navigating, and conquering Imposter Syndrome.

Although this book is gender-agnostic, it's important to note that there's still a globally reported confidence gap between men and women. Confidence also isn't one-dimensional; it's a 3D experience impacted by nature and nurture and can be demonstrated in both verbal and nonverbal ways. Over the years, several studies have examined the confidence gap and its wider implications. For example, due to a lack of confidence, women are more likely to turn down opportunities than men, harming their careers, earning potential, and life prospects.[5] One study found that women who scored equal to men on a science-based quiz underestimated their performance, knowledge, and abilities.[6] This can also play out across various STEM fields when other environmental factors come into play, as previously shared.

But there is some good news … sort of. Further research found that, over time, as women gain experience, their confidence increases much quicker than men's. By their mid-fifties, they've essentially closed the confidence gap, and by their sixties, they're generally more confident than men.[7] Great news, right? It is but … how many opportunities are women missing out on by not gaining their confidence until later in life? The impact is massive.

The 2021 Women's Confidence Report, the largest ever global study on women's confidence, adds even more to the conversation, with 11,000 respondents surveyed from eleven countries—Australia, Britain, China, France, Germany, Hong Kong, Japan, Korea, Mexico, Russia, and the US. The study used a mixture of online surveys and long-form and expert interviews to measure women's confidence in fourteen areas. It's important to note that there's a wide variety of women's experiences in this report. It's comprehensive, and it looks at a lot of cultural and social elements involved in confidence. A person's confidence is often strongly influenced by the culture in which they live, and, as we know, cultural elements and conditioning can also play a significant role in Imposter experiences. The study found that women's confidence across the world is alarmingly low, which did surprise me a little.[8] Confidence is important, and although it doesn't stop us from experiencing Imposter Syndrome, it does help us move through it faster. Only when we've conquered Imposter Syndrome can we be the most authentically confident version of ourselves, the type of person who grasps every golden opportunity with both hands and doesn't let go. Doesn't that sound amazing, life-changing even? It is.

## BUILD AUTHENTIC AND LASTING CONFIDENCE (REGARDLESS OF GENDER)

The confidence-competence loop is a powerful psychological and behavioral framework that explains how confidence and competence are intrinsically linked, each reinforcing the other in a positive feedback cycle. This loop serves as a foundation for building authentic, sustainable confidence and is particularly effective in helping individuals move on from episodes of Imposter Syndrome. By engaging with this loop, once our "Imposter masks" have been removed and we can view competence through a healthy lens, we can shift from self-doubt and fear to a place of genuine self-belief, rooted in self-awareness and measurable progress.

**The Confidence-Competence Loop**

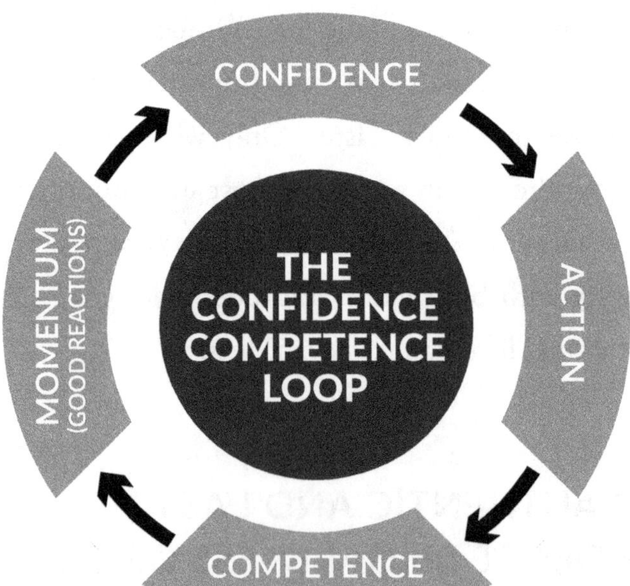


*Confidence-competence loop.*

- **Competence fuels confidence.** When you develop or demonstrate a skill successfully, it builds confidence in your abilities.

- **Confidence fuels competence.** When you believe in yourself and your ability to succeed, you're more likely to take action, practice, and improve your skills, recognizing and internalizing each step along the way.

This process creates a positive reinforcement cycle …

**Action/redirect**
We take a step, learn a skill, or face a challenge.

**Success**
Even small successes validate our effort and provide evidence of competence (which we now internalize because we have control over our Imposter Syndrome).

**Confidence**
The sense of accomplishment builds belief in our abilities and in our desire to continue.

**More action**
Increased confidence motivates us to tackle more challenges, practice further, or take on larger goals, leading to greater competence.

The cycle repeats, creating momentum toward higher levels of achievement and self-belief. The loop becomes a sustainable model for growth when individuals approach challenges incrementally, celebrating progress along the way.

The confidence-competence loop encourages us to acknowledge small successes, which means celebrating incremental achievements, such as learning a new skill or completing a minor goal. We can also track evidence of competence by writing down wins, no matter how small, to counteract the tendency to forget or minimize accomplishments.

The confidence-competence loop emphasizes using feedback—both internal and external—to enhance confidence.

- **Internal reflection** encourages individuals to pause and reflect on what they've done well, rather than immediately moving on to the next challenge.

- **External feedback** is constructive feedback from mentors, colleagues, or trusted peers. It provides objective validation of competence, especially when self-doubt clouds judgment.

Reflection and feedback allow individuals to internalize their successes, which is critical for breaking the habit of dismissing achievements or attributing them to luck. By focusing on tangible progress, individuals build the evidence base they need to challenge Imposter Syndrome's distorted narrative.

## EMBRACE THE LEARNING PROCESS

The confidence-competence loop doesn't demand perfection or even excellence; it simply thrives on *progress*. For individuals overcoming Imposter Syndrome, this means being brave enough to suck at something new—a concept often referred to as "beginner's mindset."

We live in a world that values expertise, high performance, and high achievement, so we hold ourselves to increasingly high standards ... which is OK in bursts, when not driven by Imposter Syndrome, but it's not sustainable, realistic, or healthy in every situation. There's immense power in adopting the mindset of a beginner, even for us high achievers. Now, before you think, *Alison, have you lost your mind?* ... stay with me. You've come this far.

A beginner's mindset encourages us to approach each new experience with fresh eyes, releasing preconceived notions or the weight of past accomplishments. It's about letting go of the fear of failure and being open to the possibility of *not* having all the answers.

Imagine the freedom that comes from being brave enough to suck at something new. It's liberating to acknowledge that excellence or mastery doesn't happen overnight. The process of growth involves stumbling, learning, and evolving. By giving ourselves *permission to be beginners*, we create a space where curiosity flourishes and innovation thrives. The most successful individuals (who have silenced their Imposter Syndrome) understand that the pursuit of excellence is a journey, not a destination. They view success as a continuous process of growth and exploration. It's about being "better" than they were yesterday. Small steps, big impact, with no Imposter masks skewing their perceptions of competence.

How to adopt a beginner's mindset:

- **Embrace humility.** Although humility means different things to different people, acknowledge that there's always something new to learn, regardless of your level of expertise. You don't have to have all of the answers—no one does—and people want to help you learn and succeed.

- **Learn from mistakes.** We all make them (yes, it's true, no one is perfect). Instead of letting your mistakes bring you down, treat them as valuable learning opportunities that contribute to your development.

- **Ask questions.** Curiosity fuels growth. Don't hesitate to ask questions and seek understanding, regardless of your level of experience.

- **Celebrate progress.** Recognize and celebrate your growth, no matter how small. For the extra dopamine boost, don't forget to reward yourself too. This should be a habit that continues well after you've conquered Imposter Syndrome.

Please remember that a beginner's mindset isn't a sign of weakness. It's a testament to your courage and commitment to lifelong learning. *Be brave enough to suck at something new.* Stay curious, keep learning, and enjoy the process.

## DON'T FAKE IT TILL YOU MAKE IT

It's time to retire "fake it till you make it" and other self-deprecating language. At this point, you understand the power of self-talk, not just in taking control of your Imposter story but also in sustaining high performance and confidence.

Almost everyone has used the phrase "fake it till you make it" at some point. It's commonly intended as encouragement, or as a phrase to build confidence in others. We mean no harm when using it. But the truth is … "fake it till you make it" works against you. That's because it's a form of negative self-talk, not positive reinforcement. Given that it has become such a popular and even habitual phrase that rolls off the tongue, it's a silent assassin; therefore, its true impact isn't recognized right away.

Here are three reasons why "fake it till you make it" harms your confidence and career:

1. **It's self-deprecating.** When you refer to yourself (or someone else refers to you) as "faking it," you're training your brain to believe it and discount the action you just took. The words you use to describe yourself and your actions have a profound impact on how you think and feel. You can think of words like weapons: they either serve you (or someone else), or they sabotage you. So, "fake it till you make it" is a form of negative self-talk. You're

not reinforcing your confidence; you're actually subconsciously sabotaging yourself.

2. **It triggers Imposter Syndrome**. When you already feel like you're fooling everyone or that you don't belong, imagine reinforcing that by using the word "fake" toward yourself … it's like adding fuel to the fire.

3. **You don't acknowledge your wins.** When you say, "I faked my way through it," you're telling yourself that you're not worthy of self-recognition, praise, or accolades that might come your way, which means you're also missing out on the confidence boost you deserve from taking that action. There was nothing "fake" about your accomplishment. You turned up; you delivered or performed; you did the work. Regardless of how you feel, it doesn't take away from the action just performed. The only way to build a strong baseline of confidence is to acknowledge your efforts, steps, results, and lessons along the way. You need to bank those experiences and celebrate your wins. If you don't, you risk stalling your own growth and keeping Imposter Syndrome in the driver's seat.

Now, I know what you may be thinking ... When most people use "fake it till you make it," they mean "project confidence when you're secretly nervous as hell on the inside." But just because you didn't feel confident, it doesn't mean you didn't build confidence, because confidence fundamentally is built off action, regardless of feelings. Your feelings aren't facts. The action you just took is the fact, which is why it's incredibly important for you to acknowledge the action and not dismiss it by saying, "I just faked it." Take a look at Imposter Syndrome—it makes you feel like a fraud. When you look at the facts (you've worked your whole career to gain skills and credentials, and you're experienced and very competent in your field), you only feel inadequate or unworthy.

When it comes to confidence, you may have felt like you were faking it, but you weren't. You turned up and delivered. Your feelings will eventually catch up to your actions, and your confidence will grow once you start reaffirming yourself.

**So, I encourage you to avoid self-deprecating language like "fake it till you make it" and replace it with a new true statement.**

Say hello to "brave it till you make it," a phrase shared by one of my incredible business clients, Emma. Because there's nothing fake about you or what you do.

## SUSTAINABLE CONFIDENCE = THE END GOAL

The ultimate goal of the confidence-competence loop is to foster **sustainable, authentic confidence**, confidence that doesn't fluctuate wildly with external validation or temporary setbacks. For individuals overcoming Imposter Syndrome, this means **grounding confidence in evidence**. By consistently demonstrating competence and acknowledging it, you can rebuild your self-perception on a foundation of reality rather than distorted fears.

Sustainable confidence isn't about erasing doubt entirely—it's about managing doubt in a way that doesn't hinder action or growth or have you questioning your worth. By engaging in the confidence-competence loop, individuals can navigate moments of self-doubt without losing sight of their abilities and achievements.

## CONFIDENCE AFTER IMPOSTER SYNDROME: A NEW PERSPECTIVE

Conquering Imposter Syndrome doesn't mean never experiencing self-doubt again. Rather, it's about learning how to manage doubt and rebuild confidence through deliberate action and reflection. The confidence-competence loop offers a framework for this process, helping individuals shift from discounting their accomplishments and feeling like a fraud to standing firmly in their authenticity and acknowledging their abilities. By focusing on small incremental successes and allowing competence to feed confidence, individuals can reengage with their work and life, creating new and better balance. This isn't just about regaining lost confidence; it's about building a deeper, more sustainable belief in oneself, rooted in growth and resilience. In doing so, they can move forward with renewed clarity, courage, and purpose, breaking free from the cycle of Imposter Syndrome once and for all.

So, for now, I want to remind you that Imposter Syndrome isn't your fault. You didn't ask for it; none of us would choose it, and your environment plays a significant role in its prevalence and perpetuation.

As you progress through your career, you may find yourself outnumbered. You may be the only "one," or you may be one of many. You may face people who believe you don't belong; some will even tell you. But despite what they say, you need to know that you do belong.

The question isn't: **who am I to be here?**

It's: **why not me?**

Even if you're the "first" to get where you are, you're there for a reason. You didn't fluke it. No one else was in the job interview, stakeholder meeting, clinic, boardroom, or on the stage.

You now have a choice. This is your sliding doors moment. Do you close this book, take no action, and continue to repeat the same story to yourself? Or are you ready to make meaningful and measurable change?

The power to change is already within you, and you don't need to go it alone. No one I've ever spoken to has overcome Imposter Syndrome solely on their own. I encourage you to seek out and build your support crew or be a part of someone's support crew. Your support crew can include mentors, sponsors, and coaches who all play pivotal roles in helping individuals navigate Imposter Syndrome by providing a safe space to explore their strengths, identify blind spots, be vulnerable, and gain valuable perspectives from those with greater experience. Mentors offer wisdom, reassurance and advice, while sponsors actively advocate for individuals' growth and opportunities, fostering confidence through external validation and support.

Coaches, on the other hand, and experts like me empower you with their experience and evidence-based solutions and frameworks to identify, navigate, and overcome challenges so you can surge forward and achieve whatever success means to you, tracking your progress along the way.

Beyond professional relationships … supportive networks of peers, partners, colleagues, and allies help lift the weight of Imposter Syndrome, creating an environment where individuals feel seen, heard, and encouraged to own their accomplishments authentically.

Together, these systems provide the foundation for building sustainable confidence and unlocking your full potential. So, I encourage you to define who you want in your support crew or who you can support, and take action as soon as you close this book. I wouldn't be where I am today without my support crew, and it should always evolve as you evolve.

Just by reading this book, you've welcomed me into your support crew, and for that I'm grateful. I've built the Conquer Your Imposter™ platform for you so you never feel alone and you have a place from which to get insights, learnings, tools, and the expert support you need to finally step out of the Imposter Syndrome shadow and into the light, for good.

This isn't the end of the story. It's the beginning of a new chapter, one where you embrace your worth, own your success, and show up in the world as your strongest and most authentic self.

You're not a character or Imposter in your own story. You are the *author*.

So, what's your next chapter going to be?

*Alison Shamir*

www.conqueryourimposter.com

# ACKNOWLEDGMENTS

"From my heart and soul,
I say thank you."

To my wife, my biggest cheerleader. Your support has been unwavering since day one and your belief in me unmatched. I am forever grateful and so fortunate to have you by my side.

To all who are mentioned in the book or have contributed, including the incredible publishing team at Dean Publishing, my clients, former colleagues, peers, specialists, educators, and experts, thank you for sharing your stories, experiences, knowledge, wisdom, teachings, and more. You inspire me and have helped bring this book to life. I am so happy to share it with you.

To my support crew, including family, friends, mentors, coaches and colleagues who have inspired and supported my journey in both my previous corporate life and this epic road of business ownership. You know who you are, and your impact on my life and career cannot be overstated. Thank you for your support, wisdom, empathy, compassion, leadership, advocacy, confidence, sponsorship, honest feedback, cheerleading, and more. Special mentions to Jo Gaines, Susie Moore, Gretchen Gagel, Daniel Duncan, Philip Mackertich, Roland Irwin, Julie Hirsch, Nick Tonkin, and our angel Sam Smith.

Conquer Your Imposter™ is a dream come true for me.

From my heart and soul, I say thank you.

Alison.

# ABOUT THE AUTHOR

Alison Shamir is an Imposter Syndrome expert, international speaker, certified coach, and media contributor. Through her work, she empowers global organizations, teams, institutions, and individuals with the knowledge, tools, and methods—grounded in neuroscience—they need to overcome Imposter Syndrome and present and perform as their most authentic and confident selves. She has spoken to thousands of high performers across twenty-three countries, shining a light on the pervasive but often ignored Imposter Phenomenon.

Alison is a proud member of the LGBTQIA+ community, passionate about diversity, equity, and inclusion, and is a former technology leader turned business owner.

Backed by over a decade of study and success helping others overcome their Imposter Syndrome, she combines both lived experience and professional expertise to facilitate transformative change in her clients.

More about Alison, her global work, clients and testimonials can be viewed at www.alisonshamir.com

# MY SERVICES

"Transformation begins with knowledge, but it thrives with action.

My mission is to provide both so you or your teams can unlock your true potential and make Imposter Syndrome a thing of the past."

—Alison Shamir

## SPEAKING

My keynotes combine compelling storytelling, expert insights, cutting-edge neuroscience, and actionable takeaways to engage diverse audiences—from corporate to academia to entrepreneurship and everything in between—at a deep level. My signature blend of personal and professional insights, empathy, and global expertise combined with the goal to always leave audiences with a renewed sense of self-belief and the tools to conquer Imposter Syndrome has resonated around the world.

Whether your event calls for motivation, education, or empowerment, I'll work tirelessly to ensure your audience, organization, or teams walk away inspired to present and perform at their best.

For more information on speaking content and formats, plus to view speaker videos, testimonials, and media work, please head to **www.alisonshamir.com**

## MASTERCLASSES AND WORKSHOPS

For organizations committed to understanding and dismantling Imposter Syndrome, fostering high-performing, confident, and inclusive teams, my masterclasses and longer-form workshops leverage over a decade of expertise in coaching and neuroscience-backed strategies. I design and deliver interactive sessions that help individuals and teams recognize and overcome their unique journey with Imposter Syndrome. From executive leadership teams to frontline employees, these workshops foster self-belief, authentic self-confidence, improve collaboration, and drive measurable performance improvements. Each workshop is tailored to meet your organization's needs and goals, ensuring participants leave equipped with immediately usable tools to show up as their most capable selves.

For more information on masterclasses and workshops, including content and testimonials, please head to **www.alisonshamir.com**

## CONQUER YOUR IMPOSTER™

The **Conquer Your Imposter™** platform is your sanctuary for transformation—a space where you're never alone in facing the challenges of Imposter Syndrome.

Designed for high-performing, high-achieving individuals of all gender identities, this comprehensive twelve-week coaching program provides the insights, tools, playbooks, community, and expert support you need to break free of your Imposter experience.

Grounded in neuroscience and more than a decade of expertise, Conquer Your Imposter™ is the *only* platform, program, and resource you need to truly understand, dismantle, and conquer Imposter Syndrome. This isn't just coaching—it's a complete road map to achieving and owning the success you want and deserve, thriving as your most authentically confident and capable self in both life and work.

You're only one decision away from a transformational experience.

See you inside **www.conqueryourimposter.com**

# TESTIMONIALS

*Alison's coaching was pivotal in my transformation. She helped me overcome Imposter Syndrome and become a more empowered leader. Now, I am writing a book, speaking on virtual stages with confidence, certainty, and clarity and impacting the people around me. Most important of all, she taught me to own who I am without apology. It's been life-changing.*

**—Senior Medical Doctor**

*Engaging Alison Shamir as a coach is one of the best decisions I have made in my professional career. I had been looking for a suitable mentor and when I heard Alison speak at a seminar, I was instantly drawn to her open, honest, and informed style. Over a three-month period, Alison helped me to identify events from my past that had contributed to Imposter Syndrome. I learned how to identify triggers and gained strategies to manage both past and present situations. I have been able to increase my confidence dramatically and implement specific strategies to perform to the best of my ability in my current role. I have received great feedback from my colleagues and manager on the noticeable change; it wouldn't have been possible without Alison!*

**—E-Commerce Manager**

*Conquer Your Imposter™ is a unique program. It is laid out in a particular order to take you through the necessary steps to discover and connect with yourself on a deeper level. It includes numerous modalities of instruction to help you achieve your desired outcomes. Alison is an exceptional leader, teacher, and mentor. She is genuinely committed to helping you achieve a level of success in your life that you didn't think was possible. Every week throughout the course, I could feel and see my personal growth evolving in such a positive manner. At the completion of the program, I can truly say this program is life-changing. I could go on at great length showing my appreciation and giving examples of all the things that Alison has taught me, but my one piece of advice is … if you get the chance, please, take the opportunity if it presents itself to work with Alison, as you will be forever grateful for the changes it brings into your life.*

**—Senior Educator**

*A truly transformational program. It's more than just digging into Imposter Syndrome; it made me reevaluate my values and reaccept them. This knowledge solidified my belief as a whole.*

**—Cloud Support Associate**

*Before working with Alison, I often felt self-doubt and inadequacy despite my achievements. Alison immediately made me feel understood and supported, helping me challenge negative thoughts and build confidence. Embracing the "good enough" mindset freed me from perfectionism, allowing me to celebrate all achievements. I'm very thankful for Alison's expertise and compassionate approach; her coaching has profoundly changed my life, and I highly recommend her for anyone dealing with Imposter Syndrome.*

**—Principal Advisor**

*Working with Alison has been like having someone in my corner constantly supporting and encouraging me. It's given me courage to make decisions and grow into my new role, and I wouldn't have been able to do that without her. I found it invaluable to be able to have those post win/loss discussions that derived incredible learnings for me. This work saved me from having some pointless and challenging discussions internally which could have been detrimental to my career and or relationships with peers and management. I often ask myself WWAD? (what would Ali do?) and will continue to do so. Thank you Alison for all of your support and for your unwavering confidence in me.*

**—Partner Sales Director**

*Alison's coaching on Imposter Syndrome is life-changing. I was able to unpack what my triggers were for these "attacks" of Imposter Syndrome and analyze how I would usually respond. Alison helped me recognize my "Imposter cycle" and gave me the tools to reframe my negative thoughts and stop the resulting self-sabotaging behaviors.*

**—Marketing Director**

*Conquer Your Imposter™ has been a transformative experience for me. During a particularly challenging time at work and amidst a significant life transition, I struggled with feelings of inadequacy, low confidence, and overwhelming anxiety. Alison helped me uncover its origins and I began to realize that I am enough and am genuinely successful in many aspects of my work and personal life. The tools and techniques I gained are not mere temporary fixes; they offer long-term benefits. Alison's personable coaching style, coupled with her focus on accountability, has genuinely changed my life. Now, the cycle of negative and self-defeating internal dialogue is far less frequent. I no longer spend days and nights ruminating over my actions or worrying about others' judgments. I cannot thank Alison enough for her profound impact on my journey.*

**—Financial Services & DEI Leader**

For more client experiences and testimonials head to

**www.conqueryourimposter.com**

# NOTES

# ENDNOTES

## Chapter one


1 Clance, Pauline Rose and Suzanne Imes. 1978. "The Imposter Phenomenon in High Achieving Women: Dynamics and Therapeutic Intervention." *Psychotherapy Theory, Research and Practice* 15, no. 3 (Fall). https://www.paulineroseclance.com/pdf/ip_high_achieving_women.pdf.

2 Clance, Pauline Rose and Suzanne Imes. 1978. "The Imposter Phenomenon in High Achieving Women: Dynamics and Therapeutic Intervention." *Psychotherapy Theory, Research and Practice* 15, no. 3 (Fall). https://www.paulineroseclance.com/pdf/ip_high_achieving_women.pdf.

3 Bravata, Dena M., Sharon A. Watts, Autumn L. Keefer, Divya K. Madhusudhan, Katie T. Taylor, Dani M. Clark, Ross S. Nelson, Kevin O. Cokley, and Heather K. Hagg. 2019. "Prevalence, Predictors, and Treatment of Impostor Syndrome: A Systematic Review." *Journal of General Internal Medicine* 35, no. 4 (December): 1252–1275. https://doi.org/10.1007/s11606-019-05364-1.

4 Josa, Clare. 2019. "How Is Imposter Syndrome Affecting Businesses?" *Clare Josa.* Accessed October 29, 2023. https://ditchingimpostersyndrome.com/research/.

5 Bravata, Dena M., Sharon A. Watts, Autumn L. Keefer, Divya K. Madhusudhan, Katie T. Taylor, Dani M. Clark, Ross S. Nelson, Kevin O. Cokley, and Heather K. Hagg. 2019. "Prevalence, Predictors, and Treatment of Impostor Syndrome: A Systematic Review." *Journal of General Internal Medicine* 35, no. 4 (December): 1252–1275. https://doi.org/10.1007/s11606-019-05364-1.

6 Clance, Pauline. n.d. "Clance IP Scale." *Pauline Rose Clance.* Accessed October 11, 2024. https://www.paulineroseclance.com/pdf/IPTestandscoring.pdf.

7 Jamison, Leslie. 2023. "Why Everyone Feels Like They're Faking It." *The New Yorker.* Published February 6, 2023. https://www.newyorker.com/magazine/2023/02/13/the-dubious-rise-of-impostor-syndrome.

8 Young, Valerie. n.d. "Is It Impostor Phenomenon or Impostor Syndrome?" *Impostor Syndrome Institute.* Accessed October 20, 2023. https://impostorsyndrome.com/uncategorized/impostor-phenomenon-or-impostor-syndrome/.

9 Bravata, Dena M., Divya K. Madhusudhan, Michael Boroff, and Kevin O. Cokley. 2020. "Commentary: Prevalence, Predictors, and Treatment of Imposter Syndrome: A Systematic Review." *Journal of Mental Health and Clinical Psychology* 4, no. 3 (September): 12–16. 10.29245/2578-2959/2020/3.1207.

10 Sakulku, Jaruwan and James Alexander. 2011. "The Impostor Phenomenon." *International Journal of Behavioral Science* 6, no. 1: 75–79. doi.org/10.14456/ijbs.2011.6.

11 KPMG. 2020. "KPMG Study Finds 75% of Female Executives Across Industries Have Experienced Imposter Syndrome in Their Careers." Published October 7, 2020. https://info.kpmg.us/news-perspectives/people-culture/kpmg-study-finds-most-female-executives-experience-imposter-syndrome.html/.

12 Bravata, Dena M., Sharon A. Watts, Autumn L. Keefer, Divya K. Madhusudhan, Katie T. Taylor, Dani M. Clark, Ross S. Nelson, Kevin O. Cokley, and Heather K. Hagg. 2019. "Prevalence, Predictors, and Treatment of Impostor Syndrome: A Systematic Review." *Journal of General Internal Medicine* 35, no. 4 (December): 1252–1275. https://doi.org/10.1007/s11606-019-05364-1.

13 Price, Paul C., Brandi Holcomb, and Makayla B. Payne. 2024. "Gender Differences in Impostor Phenomenon: A Meta-Analytic Review." *Current Research in Behavioral Sciences* 7. doi.org/10.1016/j.crbeha.2024.100155.

14 Jamison, Leslie. 2023. "Why Everyone Feels Like They're Faking It." *The New Yorker.* Accessed September 3, 2024. https://www.newyorker.com/magazine/2023/02/13/the-dubious-rise-of-impostor-syndrome.

15 Tewfik, Basima. 2022. "The Impostor Phenomenon Revisited: Examining the Relationship between Workplace Impostor Thoughts and Interpersonal Effectiveness at Work." *Academy of Management Journal* 65, no. 3 (June). doi.org/10.5465/amj.2020.1627.

16 Tuttle, Kate. 2023. "Oprah Winfrey Says She's Never Felt Imposter Syndrome: 'I Had to Look It Up' (Exclusive)." *People.* Accessed September 3, 2024. https://people.com/oprah-winfrey-says-she-s-never-felt-imposter-syndrome-exclusive-7968334.

17 Langford, Joe and Pauline Rose Clance. 1993. "The Impostor Phenomenon: Recent Research Findings Regarding Dynamics, Personality and Family Patterns and Their Implications for Treatment." *Psychotherapy* 30, no. 3 (Fall): 495–501. https://paulineroseclance.com/pdf/Langford.pdf.

## Chapter two

1 McKay, Sarah. 2019. "Six Brain-Based Solutions to Beat Stress." *Dr. Sarah McKay.* Published April 25, 2019. https://drsarahmckay.com/six-brain-based-solutions-to-beat-stress/.

2 Crocetti, Elisabetta, Flavia Albarello, Wim Meeus, and Monica Rubini. 2022. "Identities: A Developmental Social-Psychological Perspective." *European Review of Social Psychology* 34, no. 1 (April): 161–201. doi.org/10.1080/10463283.2022.2104987.

3 Bussotti, Camille. 1990. "The Impostor Phenomenon: Family Roles and Environment." Dissertation.

4 Scarborough, Alex. 2022. "U.S. Gymnast Suni Lee Says She's Experienced 'Impostor Syndrome' Since Winning Gold at Tokyo Olympics." *ESPN.* Published March 16, 2022. https://www.espn.com.au/olympics/summer/gymnastics/story/_/id/33509197/us-gymnast-suni-lee-says-lack-confidence-concern-following-tokyo-gold.

5 Hanson, Kait. 2021. "Who Is Suni Lee? Her Dad Shares the Olympic Gymnast's Story?" *Today,* updated July 29, 2021. https://www.today.com/parents/dad-us-olympic-gymnast-suni-lee-shares-her-story-t226398.

6 Scarborough, Alex. 2022. "U.S. Gymnast Suni Lee Says She's Experienced 'Impostor Syndrome' Since Winning Gold at Tokyo Olympics." *ESPN.* Published March 16, 2022. https://www.espn.com.au/olympics/summer/gymnastics/story/_/id/33509197/us-gymnast-suni-lee-says-lack-confidence-concern-following-tokyo-gold.

7 Hall, Rachel. 2023. "Michael Parkinson Suffered from 'Impostor Syndrome', Son Says." *The Guardian.* Published August 25, 2023. https://www.theguardian.com/media/2023/aug/25/michael-parkinson-suffered-impostor-syndrome-son-says.

8 Husock, Howard. 2022. "Honest Criticism Is a Privilege." *City Journal.* Published March 8, 2022. https://www.city-journal.org/article/honest-criticism-is-a-privilege.

9 Steele, Claude M. and Joshua Aronson. 1995. "Stereotype Threat and the Intellectual Test Performance of African Americans." *Journal of Personality and Social Psychology* 69, no. 5: 797–811. 10.1037/0022-3514.69.5.797.

10 Spencer, S. J., C. M. Steele, and D. M Quinn. 1999. "Stereotype Threat and Women's Math Performance." *Journal of Experimental Social Psychology 35,* no. 1: 4–28. doi.org/10.1006/jesp.1998.1373.

11 Clance, Pauline Rose. 1985. *The Impostor Phenomenon: Overcoming the Fear That Haunts Your Success.* Atlanta: Peachtree Publishers.

12 Harvey, Joan C. and Cynthia Katz. 1985. *If I'm So Successful, Why Do I Feel Like a Fake?: The Impostor Phenomenon. New York: Random House.*

13 Sathyanarayana Rao, T. S., M. R. Asha, K. S. Jagannatha Rao, and P. Vasudevaraju. 2009. "The Biochemistry of Belief." *Indian Journal of Psychiatry* 51, no. 4 (December): 239–241. doi.org/10.4103/0019-5545.58285.

## Chapter three

1 Harmon-Jones, Eddie and Judson Mills. 2019. "An Introduction to Cognitive Dissonance Theory and an Overview of Current Perspectives on the Theory." In *Cognitive Dissonance: Reexamining a Pivotal Theory in Psychology*, 2nd ed., edited by Eddie Harmon-Jones, 3–24. Washington DC: American Psychological Association. doi.org/10.1037/0000135-001.

2 Clance, Pauline Rose. 1985. *The Impostor Phenomenon: Overcoming the Fear That Haunts Your Success.* Atlanta: Peachtree Publishers.

## Chapter four

1 Franklin, Jess. 2018. "Imposter Syndrome: Part 1." *Monash University.* Published October 23, 2018. https://www.monash.edu/entrepreneurship/news/articles/imposter-syndrome-part-1.

2 Zimny, Thom, director. 2023. *Sly.* Netflix. 1 hr., 36 min. www.netflix.com/title/81450717.

## Chapter five

1 Journal Psyche. n.d. "Freud's Model of the Human Mind." Accessed October 15, 2024. https://journalpsyche.org/understanding-the-human-mind/; Ricee, Susanne. 2023. "Subconscious vs Unconscious: The Complete Comparison." *Diversity for Social Impact.* Published February 16, 2024. https://diversity.social/unconscious-vs-subconscious/#0-a-simple-analogy-of-unconscious-and-subconscious.

2 Huffington, Arianna. 2016. "Evicting the Obnoxious Roommate in Your Head." *Medium.* Published November 30, 2016. https://medium.com/thrive-global/evicting-the-obnoxious-roommate-in-your-head-1848db7c9d75.

3 Vaish, Amrisha, Tobias Grossmann, and Amanda Woodward. 2008. "Not all Emotions Are Created Equal: The Negativity Bias in Social-Emotional Development." *Psychological bulletin* 134, no. 3 (May): 383–403. doi.org/10.1037/0033-2909.134.3.383.

4 Barrett, Lisa Feldman. 2016. "2016 : What Do You Consider the Most Interesting Recent [Scientific] News? What Makes It Important?" *Edge.* Accessed November 18, 2024. https://www.edge.org/response-detail/26707.

5 McKay, Sarah. 2015. "What Actually IS Neuroplasticity?" *Dr. Sarah McKay.* Published March 29, 2024. https://drsarahmckay.com/what-actually-is-neuroplasticity/.

6 McKay, Sarah. The Neuroscience Academy.

7 McKay, Sarah. The Neuroscience Academy.

8 McKay, Sarah. The Neuroscience Academy.

9 Damasio, Antonio and Gil B. Carvalho. 2013. "The Nature of Feelings: Evolutionary and Neurobiological Origins." *Nature Reviews Neuroscience* 14, no. 2 (February): 143–152. doi.org/ 10.1038/nrn3403.

10 Zingela, Zukiswa, Louise Stroud, Johan Cronje, Max Fink, and Stephan van Wyk. 2022. "The Psychological and Subjective Experience of Catatonia: A Qualitative Study." *BMC Psychology* 10, no. 1 (July): 173. doi.org/10.1186/s40359-022-00885-7.

11 Willcox, Gloria. 1982. "The Feeling Wheel." *Transactional Analysis Journal* 12, no. 4: 274–276. doi.org/10.1177/036215378201200411.

12 Cascio, Christopher N., Matthew Brook O'Donnell, Francis J. Tinney, Matthew D. Lieberman, Shelley E. Taylor, Victor J. Strecher, and Emily D. Falk. 2016. "Self-Affirmation Activates Brain Systems Associated with Self-Related Processing and Reward and Is Reinforced by Future Orientation." *Social Cognitive and Affective Neuroscience* 11, no. 4 (November): 621–629. doi.org/10.1093/scan/nsv136.

13 Longe, Olivia, Frances A. Maratos, Paul Gilbert, Gaynor Evans, Faye Volker, Helen Rockliff, and Gina Rippon. 2009. "Having a Word with Yourself: Neural Correlates of Self-Criticism and Self-Reassurance." *NeuroImage* 49 (September): 1849–1856. doi.org/10.1016/j.neuroimage.2009.09.019.

14 Di Mario, Sofia, Elisabetta Rollo, Silvia Gabellini, and Lucia Filomeno. 2024. "How Stress and Burnout Impact the Quality of Life Amongst Healthcare Students: An Integrative Review of the Literature." *Teaching and Learning in Nursing* 19, no. 4 (October): 315–323. doi.org/10.1016/j.teln.2024.04.009.

15 Dweck, Carol. 2014. "Developing a Growth Mindset with Carol Dweck." *Stanford Alumni*. October 10, 2014. Video, 9:37. https://youtu.be/hiiEeMN7vbQ.

16 Moser, Jason S., Hans S. Schroder, Carrie Heeter, Tim P. Moran, and Yu-Hao Lee. 2011. "Mind Your Errors: Evidence for a Neural Mechanism Linking Growth Mind-Set to Adaptive Posterror Adjustments." *Psychological Science* 22, no. 12 (October). doi.org/10.1177/0956797611419520.

17 Santos-Rosa, Francisco J., Carlos Montero-Carretero, Luis Arturo Gómez-Landero, Miquel Torregrossa, and Eduardo Cervelló. 2022. "Positive and Negative Spontaneous Self-Talk and Performance in Gymnastics: The Role of Contextual, Personal and Situational Factors." *PloS One* 17, no. 3 (March): doi.org/10.1371/journal.pone.0265809.

18 Creswell, J. D, Janine M. Dutcher, William M. P. Klein, Peter R. Harris, and John M. Levine. 2013. "Self-Affirmation Improves Problem-Solving Under Stress." *PloS One* 8, no. 5 (May). doi.org/10.1371/journal.pone.0062593

19 Blackwell, Simon E. 2019. "Mental imagery: From Basic Research to Clinical Practice." *Journal of Psychotherapy Integration* 29, no. 3 (September): 235–247. doi.org/10.1037/int0000108.

20 Marshall, Ben. n.d. "Functional Equivalence." *Future Learn.* Accessed October 16, 2024. https://www.futurelearn.com/info/courses/mental-skills-training-sport/0/steps/147493.

21 McKay, Sarah. 2018. "7 Principles of Neuroscience Every Coach and Therapist Should Know." *Dr. Sarah McKay.* Published July 29, 2018. https://drsarahmckay.com/7-principles-neuroscience-every-coach-know/.

22 Grouios, George, Klio Semoglou, Katerina Mousikou, Konstantinos Chatzinikolaou, and Christos Kabitsis. 1997. "The Effect of a Simulated Mental Practice Technique on Free Throw Shooting Accuracy of Highly Skilled Basketball Players." *Journal of Human Movement Studies* 33, no. 3 (January): 119–138. https://www.researchgate.net/publication/331928345_The_effect_of_a_simulated_mental_practice_technique_on_free_throw_shooting_accuracy_of_highly_skilled_basketball_players.

23 Agbenyo, Samuel. 2022. "The Effect of Mental Rehearsal and Imagery on Music Performance Anxiety Among Junior High School Students." *Journal of Advanced Research and Multidisciplinary Studies* 2, no. 1 (February): 1–8. doi.org/10.52589/JARMS-9WZMUBWB.

## Chapter six

1 Clance, Pauline Rose. 1985. *The Impostor Phenomenon: Overcoming the Fear That Haunts Your Success.* Atlanta: Peachtree Publishers.

2 Young, Valerie. n.d. "The 5 Types of Impostor Syndrome." *Impostor Syndrome Institute.* Accessed November 19, 2024. https://impostorsyndrome.com/articles/5-types-of-impostor-syndrome/.

3 Badawy, Rebecca L., Brooke A. Gazdag, Jeffrey R. Bentley, and Robyn L. Brouer. "Are All Impostors Created Equal? Exploring Gender Differences in the Impostor Phenomenon-Performance Link." *Personality and Individual Differences* 131 (September): 156–163. doi.org/10.1016/j.paid.2018.04.044.

4 Sakulku, Jaruwan and James Alexander. 2011. "The Impostor Phenomenon." *International Journal of Behavioral Science* 6, no. 1: 73–92. https://www.sciencetheearth.com/uploads/2/4/6/5/24658156/2011_sakulku_the_impostor_phenomenon.pdf.

5 Sakulku, Jaruwan and James Alexander. 2011. "The Impostor Phenomenon."

6 Hewitt, Paul L. and Gordon L. Flett. 1991. "Perfectionism in the Self and Social Contexts: Conceptualization, Assessment, and Association with Psychopathology." *Journal of Personality and Social Psychology* 60, no. 3: 456–470. https://hewittlab.sites.olt.ubc.ca/files/2014/11/Hewitt-Flett-1991-Perfectionism-in-the-self-and-social-contexts-conceptualization-assessment-and-association-with-psychopathology.pdf.

7 Hewitt, Paul L. and Gordon L. Flett. 1991. "Perfectionism in the Self and Social Contexts: Conceptualization, Assessment, and Association with Psychopathology."

8 Hewitt, Paul L. and Gordon L. Flett. 1991. "Perfectionism in the Self and Social Contexts: Conceptualization, Assessment, and Association with Psychopathology."

9 Hewitt, Paul L. and Gordon L. Flett. 1991. "Perfectionism in the Self and Social Contexts: Conceptualization, Assessment, and Association with Psychopathology."

10 Hewitt, Paul L. and Gordon L. Flett. 1991. "Perfectionism in the Self and Social Contexts: Conceptualization, Assessment, and Association with Psychopathology."

11 Hamachek, D. E. 1978. "Psychodynamics of Normal and Neurotic Perfectionism." *Psychology: A Journal of Human Behavior* 15, no. 1 (February): 27–33. https://psycnet.apa.org/record/1979-08598-001.

12 Smith, Martin M., Simon B. Sherry, Samantha Chen, Donald H. Saklofske, Gordon L. Flett, and Paul L. Hewitt. 2016. "Perfectionism and Narcissism: A Meta-Analytic Review." *Journal of Research in Personality* 64 (October): 90–101. doi.org/10.1016/j.jrp.2016.07.012.

13 The Lego Group. 2024. "Girls as Young as Five Are Having Their Creativity Impacted by Pressure of Perfection and Language Bias." Published March 5, 2024. https://www.lego.com/en-gb/aboutus/news/2024/february/lego-play-unstoppable.

14 Musumeci M. D., C. M. Cunningham CM, and T. L. White. 2022. "Disgustingly Perfect: An Examination of Disgust, Perfectionism, and Gender." *Motivation and Emotion* 46, no. 3 (February): 336–349. doi.org/10.1007/s11031-022-09931-8.

15 Curran, Thomas. 2023. *The Perfection Trap: The Power of Good Enough in a World That Always Wants More.* London: Penguin.

## Chapter seven

1 Cokley, Kevin. 2024. "It's Time to Reconceptualize What 'Imposter Syndrome' Means for People of Color." *Harvard Business Review.* Published March 14, 2024. https://hbr.org/2024/03/its-time-to-reconceptualize-what-imposter-syndrome-means-for-people-of-color.

2 Stone, Steven, Chastity Saucer, Marlon Bailey, Ramya Garba, Ashley Hurst, Stacey M. Jackson, Nolan Krueger, and Kevin Cokley. 2018. "Learning While Black:

A Culturally Informed Model of the Impostor Phenomenon for Black Graduate Students." *Journal of Black Psychology*: 1–41. doi.org/10.1177/0095798418786648.

3 Stone, Steven, Chastity Saucer, Marlon Bailey, Ramya Garba, Ashley Hurst, Stacey M. Jackson, Nolan Krueger, and Kevin Cokley. 2018. "Learning While Black: A Culturally Informed Model of the Impostor Phenomenon for Black Graduate Students."

4 Stone, Steven, Chastity Saucer, Marlon Bailey, Ramya Garba, Ashley Hurst, Stacey M. Jackson, Nolan Krueger, and Kevin Cokley. 2018. "Learning While Black: A Culturally Informed Model of the Impostor Phenomenon for Black Graduate Students."

5 Stone, Steven, Chastity Saucer, Marlon Bailey, Ramya Garba, Ashley Hurst, Stacey M. Jackson, Nolan Krueger, and Kevin Cokley. 2018. "Learning While Black: A Culturally Informed Model of the Impostor Phenomenon for Black Graduate Students."

6 Cokley, Kevin, Germine Awad, Leann Smith, Stacey Jackson, Olufunke Awosogba, Ashley Hurst, Steven Stone, Lauren Blondeau, and David Roberts. 2015. "The Roles of Gender Stigma Consciousness, Impostor Phenomenon and Academic Self-Concept in the Academic Outcomes of Women and Men." *Sex Roles* 73 (August): 414–426. https://doi.org/10.1007/s11199-015-0516-7.

7 Cokley, Kevin, Germine Awad, Leann Smith, Stacey Jackson, Olufunke Awosogba, Ashley Hurst, Steven Stone, Lauren Blondeau, and David Roberts. 2015. "The Roles of Gender Stigma Consciousness, Impostor Phenomenon and Academic Self-Concept in the Academic Outcomes of Women and Men."

8 Josa, Clare. 2019. "How Is Imposter Syndrome Affecting Businesses?" *Clare Josa.* Accessed October 29, 2023. https://ditchingimpostersyndrome.com/research/.

9 Villwock, Jennifer A., Lindsay B. Sobin, Lindsey A. Koester, and Tucker M. Harris. 2016. "Impostor Syndrome and Burnout Among American Medical Students: A Pilot Study." *International Journal of Medical Education* 7 (October): 364–396. doi.org/10.5116/ijme.5801.eac4.

10 Appleby, Ryan, Maria Evola, and Kenneth Royal. 2020. "Impostor Phenomenon in Veterinary Medicine." *Education in the Health Professions* 3, no. 3 (December): 105–109. doi.org/10.4103/EHP.EHP_17_20; Deshmukh, Swati, Karen Shmelev, Lauren Vassiliades, Shasha Kurumety, Gaurava Agarwal, and Jeanne M. Horowitz. 2022. "Imposter Phenomenon in Radiology: Incidence, Intervention, and Impact on Wellness." *Patients & Practice, Policy & Education* 82 (February): 94–99. doi.org/10.1016/j.clinimag.2021.11.009.

11 National Center for Science and Engineering Statistic. 2023. "Diversity and STEM: Women, Minorities, and Persons with Disabilities." *National Science Foundation.* Accessed November 28, 2024. https://ncses.nsf.gov/pubs/nsf23315/.

12 AAUW. n.d. "The STEM Gap: Women and Girls in Science, Technology, Engineering and Mathematics." Accessed November 28, 2024. https://www.aauw.org/resources/research/the-stem-gap/.

13 Department of Industry, Science and Resources. 2023. "The State of STEM Gender Equity in 2023." *Australian Government.* Accessed November 28, 2024. https://www.industry.gov.au/news/state-stem-gender-equity-2023.

14 Blondeau, Lauren Alexandra. 2014. "The Impact of the Impostor Phenomenon on the Math Self-Efficacy of Males and Females in STEM Majors." Thesis, University of Texas at Austin. https://repositories.lib.utexas.edu/items/bf9cb08b-abbd-4321-89c9-bd6c3ccb8d3a.

15 Canning, Elizabeth A., Jennifer LaCosse, Kathryn M. Kroeper, and Mary C. Murphy. 2019. "Feeling Like an Imposter: The Effect of Perceived Classroom Competition on the Daily Psychological Experiences of First-Generation College Students." *Social Psychological and Personality Science* 11, no. 5 (November). doi.org/10.1177/1948550619882.

16 Chakraverty, Devasmita. 2020. "The Impostor Phenomenon Among Black Doctoral and Postdoctoral Scholars in Stem." *International Journal of Doctoral Studies* 15: 433–460. doi.org/10.28945/4613.

17 Jobs and Skills Australia. n.d. "Barristers." *Australian Government.* Accessed November 28, 2024. https://www.jobsandskills.gov.au/data/occupation-and-industry-profiles/occupations/2711-barristers.

## Chapter eight

1 DCEG Staff. 2022. "Neurodiversity." *Division of Cancer Epidemiology & Genetics at the National Cancer Institute.* Published April 25, 2022. https://dceg.cancer.gov/about/diversity-inclusion/inclusivity-minute/2022/neurodiversity.

2 Mahto, Monika, Susan K. Hogan, and Brenna Sniderman. 2022. "A Rising Tide Lifts All Boats: Creating a Better Work Environment for All by Embracing Neurodiversity." *Deloitte Insights.* Published January 18, 2022. https://www2.deloitte.com/us/en/insights/topics/talent/neurodiversity-in-the-workplace.html.

3 Harris, John. 2023. "The Mother of Neurodiversity: How Judy Singer Changed the World." *The Guardian.* Published July 5, 2023. https://www.theguardian.com/world/2023/jul/05/the-mother-of-neurodiversity-how-judy-singer-changed-the-world.

4 Botha, Monique, Robert Chapman, Morénike Giwa Onaiwu, Steven K. Kapp, Abs Stannard Ashley, and Nick Walker. 2024. "The Neurodiversity Concept Was Developed Collectively: An Overdue Correction on the Origins of Neurodiversity Theory." *Autism* 28, no. 6 (March): 1591–1594. doi.org/10.1177/13623613241237871.

5 Harris, John. 2023. "The Mother of Neurodiversity: How Judy Singer Changed the World." *The Guardian.* Published July 5, 2023. https://www.theguardian.com/world/2023/jul/05/the-mother-of-neurodiversity-how-judy-singer-changed-the-world.

6 Specialisterne Foundation. n.d. "Autism & Neurodiversity." Accessed November 30, 2024. https://specialisternefoundation.com/autism-neurodiversity/.

7 Cognassist. n.d. "Neurodiversity Statistics and Research." Accessed November 30, 2024. https://cognassist.com/neurodiversity-statistics-and-research/.

8 Jordan, Michelle. 2024. "Adult ADHD: Statistics and Facts." *WebMD.* Accessed November 30, 2024. https://www.webmd.com/add-adhd/adult-adhd-facts-statistics; Healthdirect. 2023. "Attention Deficit Hyperactivity Disorder (ADHD)." *Healthdirect Australia Limited.* Accessed November 30, 2024. https://www.healthdirect.gov.au/attention-deficit-disorder-add-or-adhd.

9 ADHD Embrace. n.d. "Famous People with ADHD." Accessed November 30, 2024. https://adhdembrace.org/famous-people-with-adhd/.

10 Solden, Sari. 2019. "ADHD in Women: A Symptom Checklist." *ADDitude.* Published August 28, 2019. https://www.additudemag.com/adhd-symptoms-in-women/.

11 Giordano, R. 2016. "ADHD in women: A lifetime of frustration, its cause easily missed." *The Philadelphia Inquirer.* Published 20 Nov 2016. https://www.inquirer.com/philly/health/womenshealth/20161120_ADHD_in_women__A_lifetime_of_frustration__its_cause_easily_missed.html

12 Dodson, William. 2019. "Rejection Sensitive Dysphoria: Symptom Test for ADHD Brains." *ADDitude.* Published September 20, 2019. https://www.additudemag.com/rejection-sensitive-dysphoria-adhd-symptom-test/.

13 Dodson, William. 2024. "New Insights into Rejection Sensitive Dysphoria." *ADDitude.* Published July 10, 2024. https://www.additudemag.com/rejection-sensitive-dysphoria-adhd-emotional-dysregulation/.

14 Ginapp Callie M., Norman R. Greenberg, Grace MacDonald-Gagnon, Gustavo A. Angarita, Krysten W. Bold, and Marc N. Potenza. 2023. "Dysregulated Not Deficit: A Qualitative Study on Symptomatology of ADHD in Young Adults." *PLOS One* 18, no. 10 (October): doi.org/10.1371/journal.pone.0292721.

15 Business Cloud Publishing Limited. 2024. "Neurodivergence 'Massively Underestimated in Tech.'" Published February 28, 2024. https://businesscloud.co.uk/news/neurodivergence-massively-underestimated-in-tech/.

16 Golden, Deborah, Brenna Sniderman, Natasha Buckley, and Jonathan Holdowsky. 2024. "The Neurodiversity Advantage: How Neuroinclusion Can Unleash Innovation and Create Competitive Edge." *Deloitte.* Published July 12, 2024. https://www2.deloitte.com/us/en/insights/topics/value-of-diversity-and-inclusion/unleashing-innovation-with-neuroinclusion.html.

## Chapter nine

1 Hubbard, Linda. 2023. "Behind the Mask: Managing High-Functioning Anxiety." *Mayo Clinic Health System.* Accessed September 4, 2024. https://www.mayoclinichealthsystem.org/hometown-health/speaking-of-health/managing-high-functioning-anxiety.

2 World Health Organization. 2019. "Burn-Out an 'Occupational Phenomenon': International Classification of Diseases." Published May 28, 2024. https://www.who.int/news/item/28-05-2019-burn-out-an-occupational-phenomenon-international-classification-of-diseases.

3 Villwock, Jennifer A., Lindsay B. Sobin, Lindsey A. Koester, and Tucker M. Harris. 2016. "Impostor Syndrome and Burnout among American Medical Students: A Pilot Study." *International Journal of Medical Education* 7 (October): 364–369. https://doi.org/10.5116/ijme.5801.eac4.

4 Clark, Pamela, Chelsey Holden, Marla Russell, and Heather Downs. 2022. "The Impostor Phenomenon in Mental Health Professionals: Relationships Among Compassion Fatigue, Burnout, and Compassion Satisfaction." *Contemporary Family Therapy* 44 (April): 185–197. doi.org/10.1007/s10591-021-09580-y.

5 Liu, Rachel Q., Jacob Davidson, Tamara A. Van Hooren, Julie Ann M. Van Koughnett, Sarah Jones, and Michael C. Ott. 2022. "Impostorism and Anxiety Contribute to Burnout among Resident Physicians." *Medical Teacher* 44, no. 7 (February): 758–64. doi.org/10.1080/0142159X.2022.2028751.

6 McMillan, Lynley H. W., Michael P. O'Driscoll, Nigel V. Marsh, and Elizabeth C. Brady. 2001. "Understanding Workaholism: Data Synthesis, Theoretical Critique, and Future Design Strategies." *International Journal of Stress Management* 8 (April): 69–91. doi.org/10.1023/A:1009573129142.

7 McMillan, Lynley H. W., Michael P. O'Driscoll, Nigel V. Marsh, and Elizabeth C. Brady. 2001. "Understanding Workaholism: Data Synthesis, Theoretical Critique, and Future Design Strategies."

8 Haar, Jarrod and Kirsty de Jong. 2024. "Imposter Phenomenon and Employee Mental Health: What Role Do Organizations Play?" *Personnel Review* 53, no. 1 (January): 211–227. doi.org/10.1108/PR-01-2022-0030.

9 Grant, Adam. 2021. "There's a Name for the Blah You're Feeling: It's Called Languishing." *The New York Times.* Published April 19, 2021. https://www.nytimes.com/2021/04/19/well/mind/covid-mental-health-languishing.html.

10 Josa, Clare. 2019. "How Is Imposter Syndrome Affecting Businesses?" *Clare Josa.* Accessed October 29, 2023. https://ditchingimpostersyndrome.com/research/.

11 Josa, Clare. 2019. "How Is Imposter Syndrome Affecting Businesses?" *Clare Josa.* Accessed October 29, 2023. https://ditchingimpostersyndrome.com/research/.

## Chapter ten

1 McKay, Sarah. 2016. "REFIRE: 6 Steps to Rewire Your Brain (and Master Anything)." *Dr. Sarah McKay.* Accessed December 3, 2024. https://drsarahmckay.com/refire-6-steps-to-rewire-your-brain-and-master-anything/.

2 McKay, Sarah. 2016. "How to Break Bad Habits Using Neuroscience." *Dr. Sarah McKay.* Accessed December 3, 2024. https://drsarahmckay.com/how-to-break-bad-habits-using-neuroscience-2/.

3 McKay, Sarah. 2016. "How to Break Bad Habits Using Neuroscience."

4 Solis-Moreira, Jocelyn. 2024. "How Long Does It Really Take to Form a Habit?" *Scientific America.* Published January 24, 2024. https://www.scientificamerican.com/article/how-long-does-it-really-take-to-form-a-habit/.

5 Kay, Katty and Claire Shipman. 2014. "The Confidence Gap." *The Atlantic.* Published May 2014. https://www.theatlantic.com/magazine/archive/2014/05/the-confidence-gap/359815/.

6 Ehrlinger Joyce and David Dunning. 2003. "How Chronic Self-Views Influence (and Potentially Mislead) Estimates of Performance." *Journal of Personality and Social Psychology* 84, no. 1 (January) 5–17. https://pubmed.ncbi.nlm.nih.gov/12518967/.

7 Zenger, Jack. 2021. "The Confidence Gap in Men and Women: How to Overcome It." *Zenger Folkman.* Published January 25, 2021. https://zengerfolkman.com/articles/the-confidence-gap-in-men-and-women-how-to-overcome-it/.

8 Beyrend, Morgan, Julia Colussi-Corte, Camille Jacquey, and Salomé Kennedy. 2021. "The Largest Global Study to Understand, Measure and Increase Women's Confidence." *IT Cosmetics and Eranos.* Accessed December 4, 2024. https://womensconfidence.report/.

www.ingramcontent.com/pod-product-compliance
Lightning Source LLC
Chambersburg PA
CBHW032050020426
42335CB00011B/270